GATHERING *a* REMNANT

GATHERING *a* REMNANT

LORI L. DENNING

CFI
An imprint of Cedar Fort, Inc.
Springville, Utah

Bible verses included in the text of this book are from the King James Version of the Bible except where otherwise noted.

ISBN 13: 978-1-4621-4343-6

Published by CFI, an imprint of Cedar Fort, Inc.
2373 W. 700 S., Springville, UT 84663
Distributed by Cedar Fort, Inc., www.cedarfort.com

Library of Congress Control Number: 2022938848

Cover design by Shawnda T. Craig

Edited by Spencer Skeen

Printed in the United States of America

10 9 8 7 6 5 4 3 2 1

Printed on acid-free paper

For Lisa

The Esau to my Jacob,

the Mary to my Martha,

the "Ta" to my "Wo."

ACKNOWLEDGMENTS

This book is about family, most of all. I am grateful to all of my many family members.

First, I am grateful to my parents, Allen and Lynda Denning. They not only accepted me as their daughter but they also let me tell their story. I love them. Because of them, I'm right where I need to be. I'm gathered in. Allen is strong and fierce. He loves deeply and always wants to do the right thing. He is like Jonathan. Lynda is everyone's friend. She cares for people, wants to hear your story, and loves you as you are. She is Ruth and Deborah rolled into one.

To my brothers, Mike and Rick:

While I tell quite a few family stories, I do not share as many of my brothers as I could. They are excellent brothers, despite the teasing. They taught me all the things I needed to know to succeed. I learned the importance of competitive sports. Mike taught me how to jump a dirt bike. Mike is daring and brave, and I learned to be fearless from Mike. Rick showed me how to be a disciplined triathlete. I have never seen anyone as competitive as Rick. Rick "runs the numbers" and knows every statistic, which taught me to do the same. They both put their all into everything they do—their joy, heart, and effort.

They are both faithful servants of the Lord. Rick has a testimony as big as the universe. He knows the Savior, and it shows in his every action. Rick is as obedient as Nephi and faithful as Jacob. Mike has a big heart. He loves like Jesus. He cares for his family with ferocity.

And that love and care pour out of his soul. Mike is David—a man after God's own heart.

Being a twin is the best. This book is for you. Lisa is the person who brings people together, loves everyone, and makes us feel like we can conquer the world. I want to acknowledge that this is our story, not just mine. Lisa, you are kind to let me tell our story.

Lisa is like Peter who jumps out of the boat to follow the Lord. She is like Alma the Younger, sharing the gospel with all. She is Esau, brave and courageous, forgiving and strong.

I am also grateful to my birth family. Their sacrifice and love echo on in me.

Thanks to all the birth parents, birth families, foster parents, foster families, waiting children, adoptees, and guardians, in the world. We don't even have terms for all our relationships with each other. Our paths may be complex, but our shared goal of love is simple. Thank you for opening your hearts and widening the definition of family.

Thanks to Diane Taylor, my unofficial editor, critic, and feedback expert. She has read pages, discussed concepts, and listened to me tell my story. Late into the evening, she had critiqued pages and edited content. (She pretends not to like the Old Testament, but I think she is starting to warm up to it. That alone is high praise.) Diane is the friend everyone needs, but no one deserves. She is a saint. Diane is like the prophet Jacob, a faithful soul with the heart of a poet. She is Mary sitting at the feet of the Savior. She is Nathanael the Israelite, in whom there is no guile.

I want to thank everyone at Cedar Fort Publishing and Media. They love sharing the gospel of Jesus Christ. They have been kind, insightful, and I'm grateful to Bryce Mortimer, Angela Johnson, Heather Holm, Courtney Proby, Valerie Loveless, Clint Hunter, Spencer Skeen, and the entire team. High fives all around!

CONTENTS

FIRST THINGS

I am adopted. Growing up, it was part of my personal list of descriptors. You know, the kind of checklist of how you identify yourself. I say: I'm a girl, I'm blonde, I'm adopted, I'm a twin. Being adopted was just part of my inventory of identity. I always knew I was adopted. I never remember a big discussion or "sit down with the parents" moment. Clearly, they must have told me at some point, but I don't remember the event. Being adopted was just something I knew about myself. Even today, I might mention it when I describe myself, but I might equally tell some other element of me: I'm from California, I love ancient scripture, I like dirt bikes, and I love the beach. Adoption was just there, a part of me.

Equally, I am a follower of Jesus Christ. He is my True North, my Savior, and the One I follow. At first glance, being adopted and being a disciple of Christ does not look like they have much to do with each other. Yet, my adoption story is a part of the great and marvelous story of gathering of Israel. I want to share the message of Jesus Christ and His gospel, so I want to share my story. I want to share how He has gathered me and my families.

This is my story. My attempt to explain the gathering of Israel through the scriptures might also be *your* story. I want to invite you into the account of my family, my adoption, and the Lord's hand to "gather" in my life. In the events of my life, I can see the Lord at work, and maybe you can see His hand in your life, too. The gathering of

Israel is a big concept covering ancient and modern scripture. It is also carried out one by one, as the Lord works His wonders in the world. All of us are part of the Lord's family, and He has a great work to bring us back into His presence. Bringing His children home is the gathering of Israel.

Scripture Nerd

I am a scripture nerd. I love reading and researching the scriptures, understanding how they work, learning their context, history, and languages. I started studying the gathering of Israel, and I was excited to delve into the topic, research the scriptures, and learn more.

My passion is ancient scripture, so I started my study there. As I jumped in, first referencing the Old Testament, then the life of Jesus Christ, the Book of Mormon, and finally modern scripture, I realized I needed to make the stories and references tie out, make sense, and resonate. The gathering of Israel is a vast topic found in all scripture, ancient and modern. Studying it was a bit daunting. Tying out all the stories and references was becoming a monumental task.

Let me step back for a minute and explain. When I say I love scripture, I really, *really* do. Scriptures have a unique power to invite the Holy Spirit, explain profound truths, and open our hearts to the gospel of Jesus Christ in ways that apply very specifically to our own lives. I am especially drawn to ancient scripture like the Old Testament and the Book of Mormon. Ancient scriptures can be complex, however. The time in which they are written, their language, culture, and even the length of the stories can make some of the references obscure. Tracing the gathering of Israel's critical elements through scripture was very exciting for *me.*

However, as I began this book, I read back some of the exciting verses I was studying to a friend, about tame and wild olive branches of Jacob 5, the use of Isaiah in the Book of Mormon, and my friend Diane gave me some advice.

"Lori, I love how excited *you* are. But that's not as exciting *to me* right now. Tell me why that matters to you. Tell me why that matters to me."

I sat back and realized she was right. A unique power of the scriptures is how they relate to us right now. I asked myself, "How can we take complex, ancient scripture and understand it today?" I reflected on how the Savior taught important and complex gospel topics. He used many teaching techniques. Jesus did preach directly like the Sermon on the Mount or the Sermon at the temple (Matthew 5–7, 3 Nephi 12–14). He also had many conversations and personal interactions. Perhaps His most powerful and memorable teaching was His use of parables and stories. In striving to emulate Him in my life, I humbly want to use stories to underscore the scriptures on the gathering of Israel. While I may use some familiar stories, I have also chosen to tell my own story. My story is one of lost and found, gathering and finding, and God's plan to save. The Lord has done a great work in my family, and I am guessing, in your family, too. I hope together we will see how He is "mighty to save" (Isaiah 63:1).

How the Book Works

This book has several elements. First, I want to share my story, my adoption, the story of my adopted family, finding my birth family, and the unique hand of the Lord throughout each step. In each chapter, I'll tell a part of the events that unfolded in my life.

I will also share some scriptural insights into the core elements of the gathering of Israel. We'll delve into who the gathering is for, what is a remnant, and gospel elements like patriarchal blessings. We will also review some of the themes, or common motifs and ideas weave through these stories. Identifying and tracing themes in scripture help us see the Savior and the plan of salvation in each story. The themes build and repeat so that in studying each scriptural account, we learn more about His plan to save, His plan to gather Israel.

While we do that, I'll also share some context, history, and meaning in the scriptures to help us understand and appreciate the gathering. Hopefully, these tools to understand scripture can be applied to the gathering and all scriptures. This is my favorite part, and I hope you'll enjoy it.

Studying each of these components will build on each other, reinforce the ideas, and lead us to a greater understanding of the gathering of Israel. I hope that each of the elements—my story, the scriptures, the themes, and contextual features—will weave together to help share the message of Jesus Christ and His gospel.

PART 1:
GOD'S PLAN *to* SAVE

Ramona, Gloria, and a Baby

Ramona Duran Singh Odom had lived a hard life. Raising a family in central California, she had seven children with her husband, Katha. They farmed on two ranches, raising crops as much as children. Katha's family was from India, and ranching in California was hard work. Prejudice for an Indian Mexican family was common, but sadly not the most difficult of their challenges. After having seven children, Katha died of a heart attack, leaving their family without a patriarch.

Ramona remarried Marvin Odom, and two more children came along. Gloria and Marvin Junior added to the large and diverse group of kids. They worked the fields, moving from crop to crop. Making ends meet was a full-time job. As the youngest, Gloria was a wild child without much parental supervision. Tragedy struck again as Marvin died, leaving a large and blended family without a father.

Ramona struggled to raise the children alone. Their diverse heritage, the challenge of farming, all without a father was nearly overwhelming. As if that were not enough, ownership and control of the properties were at risk. The state stepped in to help control the property management, assigning an uncle as an advisor to help run the ranch. The older family members fought for the properties, eventually pushing Ramona out. Ramona struggled to keep food on the table. She was supporting a large family and did not speak English. Just living life each day was a struggle. She had her hands full, and Gloria rebelled.

Gloria struggled growing up in such an environment. She acted out and grappled with finding a place in the upheaval that resulted in her father's death. While the older siblings tried to help, Gloria lashed out and turned to parties and the attention of young men.

It wasn't long until young Gloria, just fifteen, became pregnant. Her older siblings sent her to live with an older sister, Carolyn, a nurse in San Diego. There she could have her baby away from the judgments of the community.

This was just one more blow in a long line of distress for a family already losing their father, and then a stepfather, then their property. Despite everything they were doing to keep their family together, an unplanned baby of an unwed teen was an overwhelming final blow. What did God have planned for them? How would all this work out?

Chapter 1

GOD'S PLAN

What Is the Gathering of Israel?

The Lord is at work in the world to save His children. President Russell M. Nelson has spoken frequently about the gathering of Israel.* But what is the gathering of Israel?

The gathering of Israel is an invitation.

The gospel of Jesus Christ is the way of salvation for the world. We talk of Christ often, learning his Way, following his covenant path. We covenant with Him to become the Children of Christ (Mosiah 5:7–9). He is the way of salvation, "there is no other name given whereby salvation cometh; therefore, I would that ye should take upon you the name of Christ, all you that have entered into the covenant with God that ye should be obedient unto the end of your lives" (Mosiah 5:8). We embrace our relationship with the Savior, covenant with Him, and follow Him. We understand our relationship to Jesus Christ and work on that relationship, that covenant, each day of our lives.

Perhaps less obvious is the relationship between Jesus Christ, His gospel, and the gathering of Israel. Jesus Christ is the message. The

---

* Russell M. Nelson, "Hope of Israel," worldwide devotional for youth, June 3, 2018, churchofjesuschrist.org/broadcast; Nelson, "Sisters' Participation in the Gathering of Israel," *Ensign* or *Liahona*, Oct. 2018, 68–70; Nelson, "The Gathering of Scattered Israel" *Liahona*, November 2006.

gathering of Israel is *the way* the message is shared with the world, living and dead. The gathering of Israel is an invitation to all, living and dead, to turn to Jesus Christ and salvation.

The gathering of Israel is a reality.

The gathering of Israel is a key belief of the Church of Jesus Christ of Latter-day Saints. The tenth Article of Faith says,

> We believe in the literal gathering of Israel and in the restoration of the ten tribes; that Zion (the New Jerusalem) will be built upon the American continent; that Christ will reign personally upon the earth; and, that the earth will be renewed and receive its paradisiacal glory.

One day, the ten tribes, the lost tribes of Israel, will return. Today, we see that fulfillment as people from all nations follow Jesus Christ and join the Church. There will also be a literal fulfillment in Zion, the New Jerusalem, when Christ will reign. The prophet Jeremiah speaks of that day (and we'll cover it more fully later) when he says,

> O Lord, save thy people, the remnant of Israel. Behold, I will bring them from the north country, and gather them from the coasts of the earth, and with them the blind and the lame, the woman with child and her that travaileth with child together: a great company shall return thither.
>
> Jeremiah 31:7–8

There will be a day when the family of Israel, from all tribes and people, will return to the Lord. Like the second Exodus of Moses, we will see a great movement of people come to the New Jerusalem.

The gathering of Israel is a concept.

The gathering of Israel is also happening in our day-to-day actions in helping bring others to Christ. President Russell M. Nelson declared, "Anytime you do anything that helps anyone—on either side of the veil—take a step toward making covenants with God and receiving their essential baptismal and temple ordinances, you are helping to gather Israel. It is as simple as that."* President Nelson is teaching us that the gathering is also in the actions of spreading the gospel, sharing our testimonies, and teaching of Christ. We learn that the gathering is not only an invitation to a reality that will come but also a concept that is applied to many of the activities we participate in gospel living.

The gathering of Israel is a promise of the Lord's love.

The Lord loves us. It is easy to forget when life gets hard, or challenges come our way. Sometimes we read a scripture about people being chastened, and it feels like the Lord is far away. However, scripture is filled with the divine reaching out to us. "For God so loved the world, that he gave his only begotten Son, that whosoever believeth in him should not perish but have everlasting life" (John 3:16). The prophet Nephi evokes our most profound emotions of love and salvation, saying, "But behold, the Lord hath redeemed my soul from hell; I am beheld his glory, and I am encircled about eternally in the arms of his love" (2 Nephi 1:15).

And again, when Christ visits the people after His Resurrection, we read: "How often would I have gathered you as a hen gathereth her chickens under her wings, yea, O ye people of the house of Israel, who have fallen . . . how oft would I have gathered you as a hen gathereth her chickens" (3 Nephi 10:5).

The gathering of Israel is a doctrine that teaches us that God loves us and God keeps his promises. I love how our Father in Heaven describes His love for us (John 3:16 must be my favorite). The beautiful expression of love that the Father shows us, giving the life of His Beloved Son, is hard to comprehend.

There are times in our lives when we feel distant from God. We can feel unworthy or misunderstood. We can feel alone, desperate for help or relief in our lives. In these moments, the Father reminds us of His great love for all of us, the world. It isn't just the elect, worthy, or the life-long member of the church. God loves all of us.

---

* Russell M. Nelson, "Hope of Israel," worldwide devotional for youth, June 3, 2018, churchofjesuschrist.org/broadcasts, emphases added.

The Savior Himself tells us He can never forget us: "Can a woman forget her sucking child, that she should not have compassion on the son of her womb? yea, they may forget, yet will I not forget thee. Behold, I have graven thee upon the palms of my hands" (Isaiah 49:15–16). The Savior Himself through His atoning sacrifice shows His love to us.

Our Father and His Son love us. When we speak of the gathering of Israel, it is important to remember we are first gathered.

Let's start at the beginning.

God Has a Plan

God has a plan. From the first pages of scripture, we learn about the salvation of humanity through the grace of Jesus Christ. It is reassuring that He has a plan for the salvation of the world. When we talk about the gathering of Israel, it is easy to get tunnel vision, speaking only of the tribes, or even a smaller group, like the tribe of Ephraim. We focus on the members of the Church of Jesus Christ of Latter-day Saints, the formal missionaries, or doing genealogy work for our specific family members. We'll get there! When talking about the gathering of Israel, the place to start is not with the smallest group but with the largest. We will start with the big picture.

God loves everyone. Our Father in Heaven loves His Children and desires all of us to return to Him. You might be thinking, "What does this have to do with the gathering of Israel?" The gathering is about the Savior's plan to offer redemption and salvation to all people. Understanding that message of salvation is critical for understanding *why* the Lord wants to gather, *who* He is gathering, and *how* He is gathering. Our first step is understanding *why*.

Here's the big message: The Lord loves us. He loves me, and He loves you. He calls it His "work." He says, "This is my work and my glory—to bring to pass the immortality and eternal life of man" (Moses 1:39). The Lord's work is helping us, bringing us home. His work and His *glory* are blessing us. Glory is a powerful word. It means honor, renown, or even importance or weight.* God is saying that what brings him renown is helping us. His is full of glory by helping offer us salvation and exaltation.

Something is fantastic and humbling about the idea that God's focus is us. The creator of all things chooses to love and care for our salvation. The most powerful being in the universe, who could be doing anything, chooses you and me. He is the most loving parent. He cares for us, His children, and wants to help us, save us, and have us reach our eternal potential.

A Savior

The plan of salvation is beautiful. Before the world began, our Father made a way for us to learn, grow, and return to His presence. While we will sin and die, a Savior was provided. Adam was instructed about the plan and what to teach his children. We are part of Adam's posterity, so the instruction is for us.

> Wherefore teach it unto your children, that all men, everywhere, must repent, or they can in nowise inherit the kingdom of God, for no unclean thing can dwell there, or dwell in his presence; for, in the language of Adam, Man of Holiness is his name, and the name of his Only Begotten is the Son of Man, even Jesus Christ, a righteous Judge, who shall come in the meridian of time.
>
> Therefore I give unto you a commandment, to teach these things freely unto your children, saying: That by reason of transgression cometh the fall, which fall bringeth death, and inasmuch as ye were born into the world by water, and blood, and the spirit, which I have made, and so became of dust a living soul, even so ye must be born again into the kingdom of heaven, of water, and of the Spirit, and be cleansed by blood, even the blood of mine Only Begotten; that ye might be sanctified from all sin, and enjoy the words

* Leslie C. Allen, "Glory," ed. John D. Barry et al., *The Lexham Bible Dictionary* (Bellingham, WA: Lexham Press, 2016).

> of eternal life in this world, and eternal life in the world to come, even immortal glory. . . .
>
> And now, behold, I say unto you: This is the plan of salvation unto all men, through the blood of mine Only Begotten, who shall come in the meridian of time.
>
> Moses 6:57–59, 62

The Lord instructs Adam to teach all that the kingdom of God is available through the grace of the Savior. We must repent and turn to the Lord. God is Holy as is His Son, the Judge, and we must be holy like them to live in their divine presence. As we become new creatures in Christ, we can be blessed with this sacred nature. Then we can live eternally with them. This is the message that Adam is to teach all of us. This is the plan of salvation.

Key Ideas to Remember

- The gathering of Israel is an invitation, a reality, and a concept.
- God loves each one of us.
- God has a plan.
- The Savior is the key to the plan. Thus, we must follow Him.

Chapter 2

GOD'S PLANS *to* SAVE ALL

A Remnant

Allen and Lynda Denning had a family. They married in Southern California, had two boys, and raised them with hard work and love. Allen served in the U.S. Marines, and Lynda raised the boys and worked various jobs. Like many growing families, they worked hard, loved their time together, and had the ups and downs of life.

They loved the boys. They would have loved another child, maybe a girl, but could not have more children. The boys grew as nearly a decade passed since they started their branch of the Denning family. Despite everything they had, it felt like the family was not complete. Years went by, and thoughts of another baby surfaced from time to time. Thoughts became discussions. Perhaps adoption would be a way to find the child they felt was out there for them.

They met with the Children's Home Society of California and started the long process of applications, paperwork, interviews, psychiatric and family evaluations. They were told that adoption is a long process and not to get overly excited at the early stages. The paperwork and long wait did not dull their enthusiasm and excitement. They told everyone. They spread the news with family members, parents, cousins, aunts, and uncles. Everyone was excited for them, sharing their plans. They broadcast their plans with the Chula Vista 1st Ward. Their congregation was just as excited as they were. They even shared their dreams with their coworkers!

They could not contain their excitement for their plans to welcome a child through adoption.

The Dennings knew that an adoption—a baby—could be a reality with support from family and friends.

I have always been aware that I am adopted. While I did not know anything about my birth family, I knew that I came to my family differently from my brothers. I was adopted in a closed adoption, where the various parties and families did not know each other. That was very common then. Open adoptions are commonplace now, but most adopted families were in closed adoptions when I was growing up.

I remember our neighbor also found out she was adopted when she was a teenager. It was a tough transition for her. It changed her understanding of herself. It reset her identity. I always felt terrible for her, finding out when she was older. Not because she was adopted, but because of how it affected her. Because, for her, it changed how she saw herself, and it upset her foundation. While the day-to-day of her life had not changed, her perception of herself had.

Identity is a tricky thing. It starts with our families and us. It is how we see ourselves and reflect that back into the world. Identity and learning more about who we are fundamental to understanding our world and our place. I'm no expert in early childhood development, but knowing who you are and where you come from can profoundly impact who we are in the world.

Remember Who You Are

I think of Nephi and his family when they left Jerusalem. The trip was a challenge, with all the logistics of packing up, living in tents, and leaving behind the comforts they knew. It wasn't just material things they left behind. They were also losing a part of their identity. Before they went, they identified as Israelites from Jerusalem. Once they left, who were they? Their fundamental identity had not changed despite a physical move out of Jerusalem to a new world. Yet changing their physical location upset how they saw themselves. Nephi constantly reminded his family, specifically his older brothers, who they were. And who did he say they were?

They were a remnant.

A remnant is a special part, a scrap, a portion that the Lord saved. Nephi tells his family that as a remnant, they were of the house of Israel, the covenant people of Abraham, Isaac, and Jacob.

> Hear ye the words of the prophet, ye who are **a remnant** of the house of Israel, **a branch who have been broken off**; hear ye the words of the prophet, which were written unto all the house of Israel, and liken them unto yourselves, that ye may have hope as well as your brethren **from whom ye have been broken off**.
>
> 1 Nephi 19:24, **emphasis added**

Nephi did not start by reminding them where they grew up, their favorite sports team, or their ethnic identity. He went to the heart of who they truly were—a fragment of the house of Israel. He reminded them of who they were, not where they lived but who they were to God. He asked them to step back and view their lives as part of a larger story. He asked them to change their perspective. As a remnant of Israel, they were part of something greater. He told them who they were, "that ye may have hope." Knowing who we are, specifically to God, can change our perspective and give us hope.

Captain Moroni also went to great lengths to remind the people *who they were*. In a time of crisis, when his society was on the verge of collapse and being engulfed in war, what did Captain Moroni do? He reminded them of how God sees them. He reminded them of who they were.

Who were they? They were a remnant.

> Moroni said unto them: Behold, we are a remnant of the seed of Jacob; yea, we are a remnant of the seed of Joseph, whose coat was rent by his brethren into many pieces.
>
> Alma 46:23

Whenever the leaders of their people, from Nephi to Captain Moroni, wanted people to make a significant change, they did not focus on the goal alone. They did not just paint a picture or vision of what they could accomplish. They persuaded the people by reminding them *who they were*. Despite the risk of losing everything they knew, the Lord wanted to remind them of their true identity. The identity that the Nephites had was that the Lord remembered them. They were part of His covenant people. They were His children.

Throughout the scriptures, the Lord has saved a remnant. This common theme, this truth, starts from the very beginning of scripture and teaches us that the Lord remembers each of us. He plans for each of us, from the greatest to the smallest. He loves and has plans for all remnants, the outcast, forgotten, and broken. Even when we think we are lost, too far gone, the Lord forgets no one. He shows His love by saving a remnant and focusing on each precious child.

A key to understanding the Lord and His plans for us is remembering who we are.

Ancient Scripture

Ancient scripture is brilliant and is a work of the Spirit of God working through men and women. Thus, the scriptures are works of literary genius. We know scripture is the record of God dealing with His children (D&C 68:3–4, Galatians 4:7, Alma 30:44, 2 Timothy 3:16–17). It tells us about His purposes and testifies that Christ has His work of redemption. Scripture is also written in many literary forms. We see stories and narratives, poems and psalms, gospels, and apocalyptic literature. These different styles use different techniques to help us see God's truths and His messages. The scriptural authors use designs and themes to underscore eternal truths. Understanding the methods the scripture authors use to express gospel ideas is powerful in seeing the ideas and truths the author is highlighting.

Most of scripture is ancient. It was written by people who are unlike us in many ways. They thought about the world differently, spoke a different language, and lived in cultures very separated from our own. However, in other ways, they are exactly like us. They love, have successes and failures, and strive to understand their purpose in life. God loved them just like He loves us. While it is easy to share the same values, sorting through the language, context, and cultural differences can be a challenge. The good news is, once we do sift through all of the context and language, we see people who are just like us. As we review the big ideas, we will take a minute to look at the methods and context the ancient scriptures used.

Structure

I have to admit that structure is one of my favorite parts of scripture. In the pattern of the books, the symmetry of the poetry, and themes and motifs, I feel the beauty of the Creator. In the words, psalms, and prophecies, I see the Architect of the Universe. At first, you might not be very excited to look at the structure of scripture—and I get it. It sounds technical and boring. But I promise it has a beauty that only the Spirit can express. The structure of scripture speaks to my soul. I hope to share a little of that beauty with you as we continue to explore the gathering.

The gathering of Israel is a doctrine shared throughout all scripture. From the first page of Genesis until the last General Conference, we learn about God's plan to save. In the book of Genesis, a pattern emerges that highlights this gathering theme.

The book of Genesis is a work of literary genius. It is more than just a history, telling us about creation, the beginning of the world, and the family of Abraham. While scripture is couched in historical things, it also tells us that God has a plan for all His children. Removed from the ancient styles by thousands of years, language, and translation, the prophets' patterns to highlight the themes and ideas can sometimes be hard to see. If we can learn to spot and track these themes and recognize these literary techniques, we can see God's message.

We can see the message of scripture by understanding the structure. The structure is the pattern on which the stories are built. Like the blueprints used to plan a building, structure establishes the pattern.

Scripture structure is a lot like a quilt. Like a quilt, there may be repeating patterns of squares. Each small square has its own beauty. We see many squares when we step back, each slightly different from the next. Then we take another step back and see that all those squares form an even larger pattern.

If quilting squares are not your style, there are more analogies. Have you ever seen a photo mosaic? It is a large picture made up of hundreds of tiny photos. When you zoom in, the photos are almost anything: little animals or pictures of scenery. Together they look like hundreds of small, still images. But when you zoom out, you can see a fantastic portrait. Scripture structure, especially in the Old Testament, is like a photo mosaic or a quilt. You can see a great image or square, its beauty, and style up close. However, when we zoom out, the power of the big picture is impressive, beautiful, and sometimes enlightening.

Genesis Zoom Out, Zoom In

The book of Genesis has a brilliant structure that underscores its overall message. The book has two parts. The first part shows the big picture of God's plans. We have the story of the Creation, the fall, and the plan of redemption. We also see how people, when they follow their own paths and their own desires, cause pain and suffering. Yet, throughout it all, God covenants with His children, promises to be with them, and blesses them as they follow Him.

The first section, chapters 1–11, are a big picture view. We see big themes and truths and are seeing things "zoomed-out." We see the creation of the world, the Fall, and the plan of salvation laid out. We also see repeating patterns of people choosing for themselves, and while most do not follow the Lord, there are some highlights. We see the pattern laid out for us in Genesis. We first see God's love for humanity in creating a world for us to learn and be tested. First Adam and Eve, then Cain and Abel, the people in the time of Noah, the tower of Babel show the struggle we have to choose Him. Of course, there are high points: the patriarchs and matriarchs who will covenant and choose the Lord. We also see example after example of those who do not follow the Lord.

The second part of the Book of Genesis has a "zoomed-in" view comprising chapters 12–50. There we follow the lives of a family. The themes set in the first eleven chapters are repeated in the rest of the book. We zoom in to the lives of Abraham and Sarah, Isaac and Rebekah, and Jacob, Rachel, Leah, Joseph, and his brothers. The ancestors' stories parallel the themes and messages of the Creation, Fall, and plan of redemption. When we zoom into the story of Abraham, Isaac,

Rebekah, Jacob, Joseph, we find the same story: God's plan to save. We get real-life examples of "new" Adams and "new" Eves as the Lord works with them to help them progress, saves them, and returns them to God's presence in a new creation-Eden.

The two parts of Genesis, Part 1 from Chapters 1–11 and Part 2 from Chapters 12–50, tell the same message, albeit with different focuses. In the first part, we are zoomed-out and looking at the big picture, introducing themes we'll see through the rest of scripture. In the second part, we are zoomed-in and look at specific examples. If we start in Genesis and capture a few of the key ideas and teachings of any of the doctrines of the gospel, we can follow those themes as they develop throughout all scripture. So, the place to start is right "in the beginning."

Now don't worry. We will not read every verse of scripture and go book by the book, but we will start with a few key themes and motifs established in Genesis. From here, we can build on the glorious doctrine of the gathering. So you might be tempted to skip this point—but hang in there! Understanding the foundational ideas of God's plan will reveal the beauty and power of the gathering of Israel.

Big Themes

It's about now you might be thinking, "What does this have to do with the gathering of Israel?" The gathering is about the Savior's plan to offer redemption and salvation to all people. Understanding that message of salvation is critical for understanding why the Lord wants to gather, who He is gathering, and how He is gathering. Our first step is understanding why.

The Creation's Blessing

"In the beginning" is how the Bible begins (Genesis 1:1). While the Pearl of Great Price starts before this, I want to stick with Genesis' themes because I think it will show us something spectacular about God's plans. So, when we start the story of Genesis, God's plans begin on earth. God creates the heavens and the earth and everything in between. In seven creative periods, all earthly creation begins, including, most importantly, humanity. We learn why the Lord wants to gather us in this zoomed-out view.

First, God created things that were "good" (see Genesis 1). God even pronounces it good seven times, the final time being "very good" (see Genesis 1, verses 4, 10, 12, 18, 21, 25, 31). Here we see a Creator who creates a good world—wonderful, really—and it is made for us. We sense the great love and plans He has for us from the beginning.

The pinnacle of creation is us! After creating everything else and pronouncing it good, He creates humanity, both men and women together. We are the purpose and culmination of His design in our mortal bodies. God's creation, *including us*, is good.

Then, as if this was not enough, God tells us something unimaginable, unique, and awe-inspiring about ourselves.

> So God created man in his own image
> In the image of God created he him;
> Male and female created he them.
>
> Genesis 1:27

Did you catch it? Let's unpack this short set of verses to see what it means.

Poems and Songs

You might have missed the poetry in scripture. Modern English verse has meter and rhyme. It is also usually written indented, so it is clear that it is a poem. Songs, essentially poems set to music, have verses and a chorus. Even popular music, like rap, will have a rhyme scheme, indicating it is not prose, not a narrative, but a poem. Hebrew poetry does not typically rhyme. Instead, it uses short lines that repeat ideas.* Using repeating, short syllables, it shows ideas in parallel. Amos 5:24 highlights an idea about justice and righteousness in this poem

---

* Robert Lowth, *Lectures on the Sacred Poetry of the Hebrews*, trans. G. Gregory, 3rd ed. (London: Thomas Tegg and Son, 1835). See also James L. Kugel, *The Idea of Biblical Poetry: Parallelism and Its History* (New Haven, CT: Yale University Press, 1981); and M. O'Connor, *Hebrew Verse Structure* (Winona Lake, IN: Eisenbrauns, 1980).

But let judgment run down as waters,
and righteousness as a mighty stream

Notice how each line has a similar idea. It builds. It reinforces an idea. It draws our attention. (Like I just did with those last three sentences). While it doesn't rhyme like modern English poetry, it places a beautiful emphasis on a concept to teach us. Hebrew poetry, with its parallel verses, sometimes comparing, sometimes contrasting, is like a verbal highlighter.

Now you know what you're looking for, the highlighter of parallelism, go back and reread the Amos verse and see if you don't see it. Notice the subject of each line; judgment and righteousness are similar.

But let *judgment* run down as waters,
and *righteousness* as a mighty stream

Also, the comparison is a water metaphor: waters and stream.

But let judgment run down as *waters*,
and righteousness as a mighty *stream*

See how amazing that is? The short sentences are parallels of each other in both subject and metaphor. This kind of poetry is everywhere in Hebrew scripture, from the Old Testament to the Book of Mormon. Sometimes it may be two lines, sometimes three. Sometimes it will compare and build an idea, enticing you to search deeper for subtle nuances in the comparison. While we don't see it immediately, it gets easier with some practice. This way of expression, in poetry, increases the impact and the emotion of the idea.

In this short poem, the very theme of the book of Amos is that the Northern Kingdom of Israel should be so righteous, so full of good deeds, that it flows out of them like water. They had become fairly corrupt, especially forgetting the poor of their communities, with grave social disparity. The Lord called Amos to call them to repentance. Here we see his call to righteousness. I love the book of Amos, written to the remnant of Joseph (Amos 5:15). He calls us to return to the Lord.

Why Poetry?

There are many forms of Hebrew poetry, and by opening a page of the Psalms, you can see a few examples. Here is a remarkable fact: *the Lord typically is speaking in verse in scripture.** Amos isn't the only one. Samuel the Lamanite quotes the Lord in verse, Nephi says a lament (2 Nephi 4), and Doctrine and Covenants starts with an extensive poetry section (D&C 1). Why use poetry at all?

Some of the most significant events in our lives are impossible to express. From a profound spiritual event to experiences that evoke deep emotion, some events and experiences are difficult to capture. There are events and ideas in life that are so big, so complex, and so unique that they are hard to capture in words. They are often deeply emotional. Emotions are difficult to put into words. Events like falling in love, the birth of a child, overcoming a challenge, or a spiritual experience are all profoundly *felt*. One way we try to show our deep connection is through poetry. Think of modern music. Most of it is a love song, speaking of the powerful emotions of love and passion. Country music also expresses other powerful feelings like patriotism, the despair of losing a pet, or our desperation when unemployed and looking for work. Country music seems oddly connected to old trucks (I jest, but only a little). Scripture is the same. It uses poetry to express events that are difficult to capture in just words.

In the opening chapter of the Bible, our first poem will be an emotional powerhouse, a highlight, something we should memorize and write on our souls. Let's reread it. This time, see if you don't see a beautiful truth about God.

> So God created man in his own image
> In the image of God created he him;
> Male and female created he them.

God created men and women in *His own image*. The Creator of the universe, the God of all, the most powerful Being, created us to be *like Him*. And not just men, but men and women united. We are in His image.

---

* Robert Alter "The Art of Biblical Poetry" (Basic Books: 2011), 136.

I'll highlight some of the parallels:

So God created man in his own *image*
In the image of God created he *him*;
Male and female created He *them*.

If we knew nothing else of scripture but this one verse about the nature of God, I think we know a profound truth. He loves us. He has great plans for us. We are like Him. That idea is worthy of a poem.

Thus, in our first overview of the plan, we have the glorious truths that God created us. We are good. And He created us in His image. Why does the Lord do all of his? Because He loves us and He has great plans for us.

Who the Lord Intends to Gather

After learning about God's love for us in Genesis 1, the Creation is told again, with a different view and additional detail. In Genesis 2, we see the creation of Eden, the garden where God walks and talks with his children. We also learn who the Lords want to bless in this part of the Creation story. It might have slipped past us with so many other essential concepts. Let's turn there and answer, "Who does the Lord intend to gather in the gathering of Israel?"

4 These are the generations of the heavens and of the earth when they were created, in the day that the Lord God made the earth and the heavens,

5 And every plant of the field before it was in the earth, and every herb of the field before it grew: for the Lord God had not caused it to rain upon the earth, and there was not a man to till the ground.

6 But there went up a mist from the earth, and watered the whole face of the ground.

7 And the Lord God formed man of the dust of the ground, and breathed into his nostrils the breath of life; and man became a living soul.

> [8] And the Lord God planted a garden eastward in Eden; and there he put the man whom he had formed.
>
> [9] And out of the ground made the Lord God to grow every tree that is pleasant to the sight, and good for food; the tree of life also in the midst of the garden, and the tree of knowledge of good and evil.
>
> Genesis 2:4–9

The beginning of Creation has vital elements—critical pieces of the story. I think that's why the Creation is taught so often. In the Creation, we find the fundamental concepts of the plan of salvation. In Genesis 2, God forms the earth and heavens and then Adam. He then creates Eden, places a garden there, and two trees in the very center of Eden. The tree of life and the tree of knowledge of good and evil set our scene. These are all very familiar elements. Did you notice that it does not rain? Instead, a mist forms and waters everything. It is only later we hear about rivers watering the world, and *that* little bit of info will be critical to where we are going in our understanding of the gathering.

At this point of the Creation, the story builds in tension, and we're drawn into the events. Then, we get this odd little aside, a break, a tiny sub-paragraph that seems out of place during this critical part of the story.

Four Rivers, an Aside

What is an aside? Have you ever seen a story when there is a break in the action and one person leans over, puts their hand up to the side of their mouth, and tells some additional information? Or in modern television shows, we see a character look straight at the camera, break the fourth wall, and tell us some "insider info?" That is an aside—a literary technique that directly shares information. It is usually insightful or critical to understand what is going on in the greater narrative. That is what the next few verses are. When we first read them, they look like a strange little set of details, but they are critical information about God's blessing. Here are the essential truths:

> And a river went out of Eden to water the garden; and from thence it was parted, and became into four heads. The name of the first is Pison: that is it which compasseth the whole land of Havilah, where there is gold; And the gold of that land is good: there is bdellium and the onyx stone. And the name of the second river is Gihon: the same is it that compasseth the whole land of Ethiopia. And the name of the third river is Hiddekel: that is it which goeth toward the east of Assyria. And the fourth river is Euphrates.
>
> Genesis 2:10–14

The aside is about rivers, four rivers to be exact. You're probably thinking, "What does this have to do with anything?" Let's look at what this aside could be telling us.

Some try and place the rivers in geography. Despite the flood of Noah and all the earth being covered in water, thus changing the geography, the cities sound familiar, so we look at an actual location. The Pison could be flowing into Egypt. Havilah may be located in Southern Mesopotamia.* The Gihon is a spring of water in Canaan. Lastly, the Euphrates is near Babylon in Mesopotamia.† All four locations will be critical civilizations in the Biblical story. The four rivers are not geographically near each other; they don't even spring from the same water source.

Seeing God's hand in giving life to the civilizations of the time makes sense. The Creation story is also full of symbols. That isn't to say these events did not occur in history; rather, symbols can enhance the meaning of the circumstances. The aside of the four rivers, right in the middle of the Genesis 2 creation story, may express less of a geographical idea and more of a theological one.

The setting, full of symbols, gives this idea validity. We have two trees. Adam is created from "the dust of the earth (Genesis 2:7, Moses 3:7). Eve is "created from Adam's side" (Genesis 2:22, Moses 3:22). The symbols don't stop there. We have a talking snake. It is easy to start looking at the historical elements of the story. Yet, as we reflect,

---

* Denis Baly, "Havilah," ed. Mark Allan Powell, *The HarperCollins Bible Dictionary (Revised and Updated)* (New York: HarperCollins, 2011), 365–366.

† Baly, "Gihon," 330.

we see that symbols can deepen our understanding and the meaning God intends for us to see.

If we look at the aside with four rivers, each carrying fresh water to a major civilization, we ask, what symbolically could it mean?

Water as a Symbol

Water is a powerful symbol. It can show us life, like a spring that quenches our thirst. It brings life to the desert and humans alike. Freshwater, sometimes called living water, can symbolize The Lord and His teachings, "The rod of iron . . . led to the fountain of living waters" (1 Nephi 11:25). Water can also represent God's presence like Psalms 72:6: "He shall come down like rain upon the mown grass; as showers that water the earth." Water is also the salvation of the Lord as seen in Isaiah 11:9: "They shall not hurt nor destroy in all my holy mountain: for the earth shall be full of the knowledge of the Lord, as the waters cover the sea." Or: "Come, my brethren, every one that thirsteth, come ye to the waters. . . . Come unto the Holy One of Israel" (2 Nephi 9:50, 51).

Additional scriptures use a river or a spring as God's blessing. Let's look at the poetry example from Amos we already reviewed. In Amos 5:24, The prophet uses water to symbolize the correct actions of his people, as he encourages, "let judgment run down as waters, and righteousness as a mighty stream." The Lord uses water to symbolize His blessing, "For I will pour water upon him that is thirsty, and floods upon the dry ground: I will pour my spirit upon thy seed and my blessing upon thine offspring" (Isaiah 44:3).

Ezekiel has a striking parallel to the Eden story when he speaks of his vision of the temple, itself a symbol of Eden, and a river flowing that flows into the desert, restoring it and giving it life (Ezekiel 47:1, 6–12). John's vision in Revelation shows earth's ultimate renewal when heaven and earth meet. There is a new Eden, and the heavenly temple descends and resides again on earth. There, flowing next to the tree of life, John sees a river: "And he shewed me a pure river of water of life, clear as crystal, proceeding out of the throne of God and of the Lamb. In the midst of the street of it, and on either side of the river, was there the tree of life, which bare twelve manner of fruits, and yielded her fruit every month: and the leaves of the tree were for the healing of the nations" (Revelation 22:1–2).

The rivers flowing out of Eden, the aside, is a reminder that God's blessing was intended for the whole of creation. The water of life flowed from Eden as it flows again from the Lord. John and Ezekiel see the blessing of the Lord going to all nations, giving life, and blessing to all who will accept it. The blessing of Heaven is found in the Savior. He is the fountain of living water (1 Nephi 11:25).

> Jesus answered and said unto her, Whosoever drinketh of this water shall thirst again: But whosoever drinketh of the water that I shall give him shall never thirst; but the water that I shall give him shall be in him a well of water springing up into everlasting life.
>
> (John 4:13–14)

The first key to understanding the gathering of Israel is that the blessing of salvation through Jesus Christ is available to all people. As we examine Genesis 2, the rivers flowing out to water the earth are the Lord and His blessing; we see God's blessing is intended for all humanity. God loves all his children and invites them to come unto Him.

The vital message of the aside in Genesis 2 is that the blessings of the Savior flow out of Eden into all the world. From His presence, symbolized in Eden, the love of God is for all of His children, giving life and light. Like a flowing river, spreading to the four corners of the world, the love of God flows to all.

Key Ideas to Remember

- The Lord remembers us, even when we are separated, drifted apart, or on our own.
- He calls this separated part a remnant.
- The structure of the scriptures can help us understand its gospel themes.
- The Lord intends to gather all His children.

Chapter 3

A REMNANT

On October 28, Gloria was unconscious. She had carried her baby to near full term. It had been a very emotionally challenging time. She was a pregnant teen, away from home for the first time, apart from family and her boyfriend Dale. The pregnancy had been emotional and complex, living apart from everything she knew. Where would she live? How would she support this baby?

She lived with her sister Carol, and both were still trying to work out how to raise the child. As a teenager, Gloria had few resources. Her sister, Carol was only twenty-two years old and trying to find a small house they could buy to try and support Gloria and the child. At this point, sonograms were not yet common, so the gender of the child was still unknown.

What was also unknown was that Gloria was carrying twins girls. She also had complications, including high blood pressure, nausea, and blurry vision. As the due date grew near, Gloria's health declined rapidly. She had preeclampsia and was in severe medical distress. Carol arrived home to their shared apartment to find Gloria unconscious on the floor.

Rushed to Mercy Hospital in San Diego, Gloria delivered not one baby girl but twins. She named them Desiree and Dawn.

Does the Lord Remember Me?

It is hard sometimes to feel special. When we read the stories in scriptures of great events and miracles, it is easy to see those blessings reserved for others. Maybe, we think, God worked differently in the past, with miracles and wonders. It seemed He worked with unique people—people not like us. We're just . . . normal. When we look around, it is easy to see the prophets and saints, like Nephi, Alma, Miriam, Mary, Joseph Smith, and Russell M. Nelson, seeing visions and working with the Lord directly. But sometimes, those people seem unique and different than us. In those moments we ask, "Does the Lord remember me, too?"

The Lord answers that question in the scriptures. Throughout history, the Lord has saved a remnant. He has worked His wonders using the smallest group, even a single individual. While it is easy to see the big movement of history, it is often in the smallest group, the single individual that He works His miracles.

It is easy to think of examples when God showed His power to many. The Lord parted the Sea during the Exodus, and Moses led the Israelites through the sea on dry ground (Exodus 14:21–31). And the Savior Himself showed great power to thousands when he fed five thousand with just five loaves and two fish (Matthew 14:13–21). Or perhaps we recall the vision, a series of visions of the Son, insights into the celestial realms that were viewed in our dispensation (D&C 76). These miracles and events may seem the typical way the Lord works with us. However, when we look closely, we see that often, those that follow Him are a small group.

Moses started life as just a baby, an adopted child, placed in an ark in a river. And Joseph Smith was a poor farm boy who wanted to learn more about the Lord. Each of these miracles started with something small and seemingly insignificant. Being chosen—an idea we'll talk about shortly—usually starts with being small, overlooked, and atypical.

The Lord often starts with the smallest group or an individual. Being a believer has often meant we are in the minority. Giving humanity our agency, our ability to choose, results in many people choosing poorly. Also, we live in a fallen world. Thus, we can find war, poverty, and injustice across all cultures in nearly every generation of time. Surrounded by evil, we may look around and wonder how God will protect us in such trying times. As we turn to scripture, we see this reality play out, as a small group of faithful are protected by the

Lord. Rather than work with big groups, showing miracles to millions at once, the Lord often works one on one. Working with one family or one person at a time, the Lord starts with the smallest fragment of society. These families, these individuals, are the spark the Lord uses to ignite a fire of change. These are remnants.

Noah, a Remnant

One of the first examples is in the story of the prophet Noah. Noah lived in a time when all the world had grown wicked. "And God saw that the wickedness of men had become great in the earth; and every man was lifted up in the imagination of the thoughts of his heart, being only evil continually" (Moses 8:22). Then we know the story. The flood comes and destroys every living thing, except the family of Noah and the animals on the ark. While the word "remnant" does not appear in the verses, we see the concept of a remnant being saved.

> And every living substance was destroyed which was upon the face of the ground, both man, and cattle, and the creeping things, and the fowl of the heaven; and they were destroyed from the earth: and Noah only remained alive, and they that were with him in the ark.
>
> Genesis 7:23

In our zoomed-out view in Genesis, we again see an idea, a theme set up that will carry through scripture. The theme of a remnant being saved. Despite the "de-creation" of the flood, God saves Noah and his family from destruction.

Why did Noah and his family survive? When everyone else in this generation was evil, why did the Lord save Noah? Moses 8:13, "And Noah and his sons hearkened unto the Lord, and gave heed, and they were called the sons of God." We get a key for our lives in just a few short words. When challenges, even evil, surround us, we should also "hearken unto the Lord." We listen, and we follow. As we do so, we become His children.

That is it! We get one sentence. We don't know much else. We don't hear about Mrs. Noah and their family. We don't hear about what challenges they had and if they participated in Family Home

Evening or family "Come, Follow Me" scripture study. There is no story about Noah growing up, Mrs. Noah serving a mission, or their kids learning about the Lord. As we approach these stories, we notice that there is little detail. If anything, it jumps out at us that the specifics are scarce. We don't always have answers about why things are happening, what motivated the people, and how they all worked out. Yes, there are a few vital details, but we have more questions than answers. And that is by design.

When we approach scripture stories, we are invited into them.

Scripture as an Invitation

Scriptures have power each time we return to them. Feasting on scripture is not about reading or hearing them once, instead, it is in returning to them again and again. We can find the Lord there when we engage with the stories. One key to accessing the power of the Lord is understanding what we bring to it. We are part of the scriptural experience. Scripture requires that we engage and open our hearts and souls to the events. Sure, we read the story for its history. We can read about ancient people and examine, as if from a distance, how the Lord worked with them. There is, however, a power in scripture that is deeper than just reading. We have to get personally involved with the text to feel more impact. Nephi explained that in teaching scripture to his family, he did "liken all scripture unto us" (1 Nephi 19:23). Scripture can become truly powerful when we dive in with our minds and hearts.

By seeing ourselves in the text, imagining ourselves in each story, in every character, we start to experience the Lord through their experiences. Sure, we can just read the story and move on, but when we immerse ourselves in it, ask ourselves what we would do and how we would feel, we unlock another layer of meaning. Oh, but it is hard to do. The scriptures ask us to do more than just read. They ask us to open our hearts and look inside—even the dark and scary corners. We must allow ourselves to hope, believe, and have faith.

This level of delving into the scripture can be terrifying, emotionally revealing, and we may find ourselves feeling vulnerable. Yet here, when we move *into* the stories, we can meet the Lord where he met those ancient people. He can speak to our souls the way he worked with them. The joy they felt, the communion with Him, can be ours if we open ourselves to Him. If we do the work, ask the tough questions, and allow ourselves into their stories. And there He can meet us.

How to Liken the Scriptures

One key is repetition. When we read a scripture story, the story itself has not changed, has it? How many times have we started the Book of Mormon and read the story of Nephi and his family? I bet most of us can quote the introduction, "I Nephi, having been born of goodly parents . . ." The facts of the story are not new. So, why read it over and over again? Here's the key: because we are not the same people. Each time we read and reread the story, we are different. It might only be a week later, but that week of our lives has changed us. What if it is years between reading? We may be in a whole different part of our lives, and we bring ourselves into the events of scripture!

The first time we hear the stories, we may learn about people and their faith, challenges, and lives. We start with the facts of the story the first time around. We understand the people, places, and events of the story. This first pass at an account, we learn the plot—the details of who, what, and when. We also know about how the Lord worked with them in their lives. Later, we start to see ourselves in them. We return to them again, and we start to see our own lives in theirs. Again and again, we return to the same stories, and we can see something new. We bring ourselves into the story, and we are different from the last time we engaged.

The scriptures can be different because we are different each time we return. Our lives have changed, and we might not be the same people we were when we first read them. We have gotten older; our role may have changed. First, we were children, and now we may be parents or grandparents. Perhaps we have had a tremendous personal tragedy, and those scriptures have new meaning for us. Maybe we have experienced the Lord's tender mercies and rejoice with the scriptures showing His blessing. We can see ourselves reflected in them. And each time we return, we can see new insights and applications.

Thus, the power of the scriptures is not learning a new plot detail or a new historical insight. The power of scripture is its ability to change us. To access this change, we have to engage with the stories. We must bring our hearts to the events. The key is opening ourselves to the stories, the people, and the circumstances in them. Their stories can become our stories. The Lord works through those stories through the Holy Spirit. He shows us new insight, a new application. We feel and experience added depth and application. We can emerge from the scriptures as a changed person.

Okay, enough about how to read scripture for a minute. Let's get back to God's plan to save.

A Remnant Saved to Restore Others

The salvation of Noah and his family sets the idea that the Lord saves a tiny remnant. The Lord will use that remnant to save others. For Noah, his family begins the story again. They are a re-creation, a "redo" of the creation story, adding this element of a remnant. In the story of the flood and salvation of Noah and his family, a pattern is set. The pattern of a remnant the Lord will save.

If Noah sets the pattern of a remnant, what other patterns and concepts are set there that we will see over and over in scripture? So, head back into the story of Noah. We started that a few pages ago, but there is more to uncover. Returning to the beginning of Genesis, we build on the themes with the story of Noah. Found in our first section is the zoomed-out view. Many of the themes and ideas which are told in Genesis 1–11 will be built on, repeated, and re-examined in later scripture. We have already surveyed the idea of the plan of salvation and God's plan for all His children. Specifically, we looked at the river of the life of the Lord flowing to all the world. Now, we turn to a story of de-creation and recreation. Noah is a story of a reset.

Adam and Eve, Noah, Lightning Round Quick Review

After the Lord had created all things, He created humanity. As the culmination of His creation, man and woman together were made in His image (Genesis 1). Then humanity was deceived, chose the tree of knowledge of good and evil, and was banished from the garden (Genesis 2). A Savior was to be given to provide salvation from sin and death. "And I will put enmity between thee and the woman, and between thy seed and her seed; it shall bruise thy head, and thou shalt bruise his heel" (Genesis 3:15). The Lord promises Adam and Eve and all humanity that there is One who will overcome the evil of the serpent. The Snake Crusher will be born, a child of Eve. While the snake, its very head, will be crushed, it will still bruise His heel. We know that the promised Son will finally defeat the snake. This is Jesus, of course! The Lord will suffer and die, but ultimately redemption of humanity will come through Him.*

The story of Genesis continues with the hope that humanity will turn to God but sadly many examples of the opposite. First Cain, then one after another, humanity listens to the deception of the snake. Eventually, we hear of Noah.

Noah, his name means "rest."† In Noah, we see a pattern of a new creation and a new hope for humanity. Here we hope to have the "rest" that the Lord offers. Perhaps in Noah and his family, we will return to Eden and the presence of the Lord. Perhaps now humanity will enter the Lord's rest.

After generation after generation of violence and sin, a prophet is born, and we begin to hope. We hear, "And Noah and his sons hearkened unto the Lord, and gave heed, and they were called the sons of God" (Moses 8:13). Noah isn't the only righteous person. We have met Adam and Eve, Abel, Seth, and others. Yet here, in our zoomed-out view, we pause on this story.

---

* John H. Sailhamer, *The Pentateuch as Narrative: A Biblical-Theological Commentary* (Zondervan Academic: 1995), 108.

† Brown, S. Driver, and C. Briggs, *The Brown-Driver-Briggs Hebrew and English Lexicon* (Boston: Hendrickson Publishers, 2004), 215 and 2022. See also entry 5146.

Noah's story is worthy of its own book. The themes and ideas explored in the Noah story teach of Christ and the plan of salvation. While we won't have time to give it the proper attention, we can at least remember the basics of the story

The world has continued to choose wickedness. Violence has overtaken creation, "And God saw that the wickedness of men had become great in the earth; and every man was lifted up in the imagination of the thoughts of his heart, being only evil continually. . . . The earth was corrupt before God, and it was filled with violence" (Moses 8:22, 28). As a result, the flood is prophesied. And amid all the evil, corruption, and sin that people have embraced, the Lord teaches us a vital lesson.

He will save a remnant.

> And every living substance was destroyed which was upon the face of the ground, both man, and cattle, and the creeping things, and the fowl of the heaven; and they were destroyed from the earth: and Noah only remained alive, and they that were with him in the ark.
>
> Genesis 7:23

The family of Noah is saved, and humanity is saved through them. This essential truth, this theme, that the Lord remembers even the smallest group is vital. Over and over, we will see the Lord reaching down and saving a remnant. And He will use that remnant to help share the gospel and save the world.

Nephi, Another Remnant

It isn't just in the Old Testament that the Lord saves a remnant. There are many notable remnants that He saves from physical and spiritual destruction, so they can bless and save others. Have you guessed who it might be? This remnant we know, perhaps more than any other ancient covenant people, the Nephites.

Nephi's Vision

In the glorious account of Nephi's vision, he sees the future. In 1 Nephi 13, he recounts a thrilling view into the world's future. Making it even more impressive, it is our past. Thus, as we progress in the vision of event after event, Nephi is shown the highlight of the Book of Mormon: the Savior visiting the Americas. Here is the climactic visitation of the Savior. During this future visit, the Lord called the Lehites (Nephites and Lamanites) a remnant.

> Behold, saith the Lamb of God, after I have visited a remnant of the house of Israel—and this remnant of whom I speak is the seed of thy father— . . . I will be merciful unto the Gentiles.
>
> 1 Nephi 13:34

Here again, we see the idea that the Lord has saved a fragment of a society, a remnant, and they will become a tool to save many others.

When we think of the story of the Nephites, it may seem like a tragedy. As a remnant, Lehi and his family are saved out of Jerusalem at a time of great wickedness and destruction. They are led to a new land and prosper, as the Lord blesses them. The Nephites covenant with Him and even are blessed with a visit by the Resurrected Christ. But wickedness and apostasy overwhelm the righteous remnants until only the wicked remain. This is the story of the Book of Mormon. How does this remnant, who is destroyed, help save others?

Think of the impact of the Book of Mormon, the result of the remnant of Lehi, which is the keystone of our religion! This book of scripture shares the covenants and promises of the Lord. In it, we find the salvation of not just the current members of The Church of Jesus Christ of Latter-day Saints. The Book of Mormon is a conversion tool to bring others to Christ. Elder David A. Bednar said, "The Book of Mormon is another testament of Jesus Christ and the great tool of conversion in the latter days. Our purpose in sharing the gospel is to invite all to come unto Jesus Christ, receive the blessings of the restored gospel, and endure to the end through faith in the Savior."*

---

* David A. Bednar, "With the Power of God in Great Glory," *Liahona*, October 2021.

Through the remnant of Lehi and through the testimony of the Savior in the Book of Mormon, those living and dead will have the words of salvation. The title page summarizes this glorious goal,

> Which is to show unto the *remnant* of the house of Israel what great things the Lord hath done for their fathers; and that they may know the covenants of the Lord, that they are not cast off forever—And also to the convincing of the Jew and Gentile that Jesus is the Christ, the Eternal God, manifesting himself unto all nations.
>
> Title Page, Book of Mormon, emphasis added

There are so many things to highlight. First, the family of Lehi is a remnant! Like Noah and so many other groups, the entire family—including Lamanites and Nephites—are the method the living and dead will have the words of salvation. The Book of Mormon will help show back to another remnant the covenants of the Lord. We will learn that Jesus is the Christ through the work of the remnant of the family of Nephi.

Joseph of Egypt

Joseph's story is one of exile, being a remnant, and restoration. His story is a perfect similitude of the gathering of Israel. Here, at the final few chapters of the Book of Genesis, we see a theme critical to understanding God's plans. We find ourselves at the end of the story of Joseph and his brothers. Joseph is Abraham and Sarah's great-grandson. As one of the twelve sons of Jacob, also called Israel, his story becomes our story.

Joseph in Egypt is one of the longest single narratives in scripture.* It is a small book, a novella, following the life of Joseph. When we first meet Joseph, he is Jacob's favorite son. As the only son of his favorite and beloved wife, Rachel, Jacob showers affection and favor

* Roger D. Aus, "Jesus as a Nazirite in Mark 14:25 PAR., and Joseph's Reunion Meal in Judaic Tradition," in *Searching the Scriptures: Studies in Context and Intertextuality*, ed. Craig A. Evans, Jeremiah J. Johnston, and Chris Keith, vol. 543, Library of New Testament Studies (London; New Delhi; New York; Sydney: Bloomsbury T&T Clark, 2015), 83.

on Joseph. Jacob will have another son by Rachel, baby Benjamin, but at the beginning of this story, Joseph is Rachel's only child. Jacob loved Rachel and worked fourteen years to earn her hand (Genesis 29:18–30). Jacob has many sons, and they are jealous of Jacob's affection for this youngest brother. Jacob, later named Israel, causes strife among his children by showing extra favor. It says,

> Now Israel loved Joseph more than all his children, because he was the son of his old age: and he made him a coat of many colours. And when his brethren saw that their father loved him more than all his brethren, they hated him, and could not speak peaceably unto him.
>
> Genesis 37:3–4

Jacob showed young Joseph great favor and gave him a special coat. This favor, as well as Joseph's prophetic dreams, do not endear him to his older brothers.† Joseph shares with his older brothers his dreams of being a ruler and others, even them, bowing down to him in obeisance. Joseph's brothers do not appreciate his gifts and they become extremely jealous. So much so, they plot to kill him. They throw him in a pit to await his fate. Later, Reuben, the oldest, convinces them not to kill him, and Judah, Leah's fourth son, convinces them to sell him as a slave.

The brothers plan Joseph's sale and the deception of their father Jacob. They lie and show Jacob that Joseph was killed by wild animals. They take the coat, dip in the blood of a goat, to complete their ruse. Jacob laments the destruction of his beloved son.

Joseph is sold and carried off to be a slave in Egypt. While there, he falls even further, being imprisoned on trumped-up charges. In prison, he can interpret the dreams of two of Pharaoh's servants. His gift of dream interpretation is a blessing. Eventually, Joseph interprets Pharaoh's dreams of an upcoming famine.

Joseph, the dreamer, is finally vindicated. The Pharaoh promotes Joseph as an officer in the court, responsible of planning for

---

† V. Matthews, "The Anthropology of Clothing in the Joseph Narrative," *JSOT* 65 (1995): 25–36.

his prophesied famine. Joseph saved grain for all of Egypt, saving his adopted nation through his prophetic gifts.

Back in Canaan, his brothers have fallen on hard times. The famine has struck them, too. In desperation, they set out for Egypt, where they hear there is grain. They are still completely unaware Joseph is there, in charge, and responsible for the surplus.

When the brothers arrive to ask for grain, it is Joseph they meet. They do not recognize him! Joseph decides to wait to reveal himself as their brother, instead deciding to test them. Have they grown and matured from the men who had sold him? After a number of tests, Judah, the brother who contrived to sell him, offers himself as a ransom for Benjamin, the youngest.

In a turn of events, Judah, the brother who sold Joseph when he was the youngest brother, now offers his own life for the youngest. Joseph now knows they are not the same men he knew so long ago. He finally reveals himself to them in a dramatic scene.

> 4 Then Joseph said to his brothers, "Come closer to me." And
> they came closer. He said, "I am your brother, Joseph, whom
> you sold into Egypt. 5 And now do not be distressed, or angry
> with yourselves, because you sold me here; for God sent me
> before you to preserve life. . . .
>
> 7 God sent me before you to preserve for you a remnant on
> earth, and to keep alive for you many survivors. 8 So it was
> not you who sent me here, but God. . . .
>
> 12 And now your eyes and the eyes of my brother Benjamin
> see that it is my own mouth that speaks to you. 13 You must
> tell my father how greatly I am honored in Egypt, and all
> that you have seen. Hurry and bring my father down here."
>
> 14 Then he fell upon his brother Benjamin's neck and wept,
> while Benjamin wept upon his neck. 15 And he kissed all his
> brothers and wept upon them.
>
> Genesis 45:4–6, 7–8, 12–15 NRSV

Joseph's story is profound in its symbolism. The chosen of the Lord, gifted with dreams is exiled. Joseph is an exile, scattered. He is separated from his family, his home, the love of his father, and all the blessings he expected. Joseph's blessings of family, prosperity, and a promised land are stripped from him by his own brothers.

Yet, in a dramatic fashion, the Lord restores all of Joseph's covenant blessings. Joseph sees greater purpose in the events of his life. "God sent me before you to preserve for you a remnant on earth," he says (verse 7). Instead of misery and slavery, Joseph sees his exile and scattering as a blessing. He was a remnant, saved aside so that he could bless his whole family and a nation.

Many Remnants

We have just examined three stories of remnants. There are many of them. We'll discuss a few examples in detail, but for now, what other examples can you think of?

A striking example of a remnant who will save others is Moses. His story starts as a tiny remnant, a baby in an ark, saved from Pharaoh, only to return and bring salvation to all of Israel. It is not just men who are examples of being a remnant but women like Ruth, a convert, saving one family that will eventually be the family line of Jesus himself. Or Esther, who saves her whole nation from destruction. Think about Alma the Younger, being rescued from his misguided life to become the prophet and teacher of a nation.

Consider Joseph. Which Joseph? It seems like all the men named Joseph follow this pattern. We have already looked at Joseph of Egypt, but there are more Josephs that follow the pattern. What about Joseph, Mary's husband? Joseph helps save the baby Jesus and Mary, so her son can redeem the world. Perhaps one of the greatest remnant stories of Joseph: Joseph Smith, who becomes the vehicle of the Restoration, restoring covenants and teachings of the Savior, to ultimately assist in saving all generations, living and the dead.

There are many, many remnants in scripture. All, of course, points to the One, the Savior of the world, who leaves His celestial throne to descend to earth, to save each of us. He is the true remnant who saves.

I hope we start to see the theme of a remnant. Once we see it, we begin to see it everywhere. Indeed, the Lord has a plan to redeem His children, and using a remnant is a common way to do it. While there are so many things to discuss, let's review what we've learned so far.

Key Ideas to Remember

- The Lord loves His children and desires to save and bless them.
- We often struggle, sin, and lose our way.
- When all looks lost, the Lord begins again to save them, starting with a small group.
- The small group, a remnant, is sent to a new place.
- While experiencing their own troubles, the remnant becomes the source of salvation for others.
- The Lord blesses the remnant as they turn to Him in covenant and obedience. He saves a portion He uses to give life, blessing, and salvation to the world.

Chapter 4

The COVENANT

Years ago, I had a missionary farewell. I think they call them "speaking in sacrament meeting" now. But when I was preparing to go on a mission, my home ward in Chula Vista, California, let me speak. This was going to be my big moment in my church life. It seemed like a big deal to me then. I was a young adult, had been away at college, and was going to talk about my mission, or my insights on spiritual things, in front of all my friends, congregation, and family. It was my moment to shine!

I was thrilled. Yes, I am one of those rare individuals who loves public speaking. Give me an opportunity to say something, and I'll take it. I even studied public speaking in college, was on the speech team, and felt pretty good about my ability to entertain and teach. I had graduated from seminary, gone to Institute, and had hundreds of scriptures memorized. I knew all the answers to the big questions. At least, I thought I did.

In short, I was an arrogant kid. But who isn't at that age?

Preparing for weeks, I carefully chose my missionary plaque scripture, "Oh that I was an angel" (Alma 29:1). I invited friends and family. Semo, a family friend, offered to sing a version of the scripture. My carefully crafted farewell was going to be a spiritual masterpiece. I was so convinced that this would be an event to remember that I even invited old high school teachers who had remained friends of the family. Some of my Jewish friends came. I had other friends from different Christian denominations coming to support me. This was going to be my big moment! As I lay in bed in the evenings leading up to the day, I would imagine myself giving the perfect talk—a sermon, really—and my friends and family weeping with my insights.

I can't believe I'm even sharing this; it is so embarrassing. But there is a point, and we're getting to it.

I distinctly remember speaking but cannot remember anything I said or any topics that I had prepared. Not really. However, there was one point when I remember stumbling over thought and pausing. I was talking about being called to serve, and it hit me, "This isn't about me at all." The silence dragged out for what seemed an eternity, and I said—the only part of my talk I still remember—"I guess I don't know why I had to wait to be called to Spain to serve people." That phrase, that idea, has stuck in my head for decades.

If I had been blessed with so many things—from family to education to the gospel of Jesus Christ—why was I just now figuring out that I was given all of that so that I could help others? If Jesus Christ, my exemplar, was about serving and uplifting others, why did it take an invitation from a prophet of God to think of someone besides myself?

That idea that we are blessed so that we can serve others as Jesus would serve is part of what it means to make a covenant.

What Is a Covenant?

Speaking of a covenant, President Russell M. Nelson said, "It is a sacred promise with God ."* When we speak of covenants, we often use legal language like "it is like a contract" or "it is an agreement between multiple parties." While those ideas are correct, they lose the impact of what a covenant with the divine truly is.

Relationship

A covenant is a promise of a relationship. A covenant is an agreement the Lord makes with us. In short, the Lord uses covenants to bind Himself to us. It feels like He wants us to know that He will never leave us. The Savior will always be there. The Lord covenants

* Russell M. Nelson, "Covenants," *Liahona,* October 2011.

to bless us, bring us close, protect, and love us. A covenant means that God, the Ruler of the Universe, is aware of and deeply concerned with our welfare. He wants to love and teach us, and with a covenant, He promises always to do so. President Nelson underscored this idea when he said, "One of the most important concepts of revealed religion is that of a sacred covenant."†

God Sets the Terms

God sets the terms of the covenant. This is fundamental and critical to understanding how covenants work. We do not put the Lord under a covenant. He sets the rules. We often think of a covenant as a two-way contract between the Lord and us. There are many individual covenants that we have requirements AND shockingly, there are a few examples of the Lord covenanting with humanity and no obvious requirement from us! God's covenant is with Noah and all living creatures. God promises to refrain from destroying the earth with water (Genesis 9:8–17). Noah, humanity, and the animals do not have to do anything in this covenant. This example spotlights the idea that covenants start with God's terms. He is putting Himself under "contract."

If the Lord sets the rules, then He can also require something from us. As God promises us many blessings, He often fixes terms of obedience and faith that we must obey to secure the Lord's promises. While the Lord promises to never leave us, we must be faithful and obedient to ensure the promised blessings. Read these next verses and listen for Christ's strident promises to us because He loves us. He binds himself to us, asks us to do something, to save us.

> [8] And again, I say unto you, I give unto you a new
> commandment, that you may understand my will
> concerning you; [9] Or, in other words, I give unto you
> directions how you may act before me, that it may turn to
> you for your salvation. [10] I, the Lord, am bound when ye
> do what I say; but when ye do not what I say, ye have no
> promise.

---

† Nelson.

Doctrine and Covenants 82:8–10

Being in a relationship is more than a contract. It is something deeply felt. We commit ourselves utterly—heart and soul—to our most important relationships. We give, serve, and think of the other first. A covenantal relationship with the Savior is no different. When He promises to covenant with us, He is bound to us in ways we cannot understand. Remembering this relational aspect of a gospel covenant makes it easier to desire to be better. We feel His commitment and we want to serve, obey, and learn. Obedience becomes something that pours out of us, not because of obligation, but because of love. "We love Him, because He first loved us" (1 John 4:19).

The Covenant of a Savior

The greatest blessing we can receive from the Lord is the promise of salvation through the Savior Jesus Christ. The primary, fundamental, most important, key promise we are given of any covenant is the promise of the Savior. It is the primary covenant promise we receive as children of the covenant, "The Father having raised me up unto you first, and sent me to bless you in turning away every one of your from his iniquities; and this is because you are the children of the covenant" (3 Nephi 20:26). The Lord makes His covenant with us and recalls that bond.

> 29 And I will remember the covenant which I have made with my people; and I have covenanted with them that I would gather them together in mine own due time, that I would give unto them again the land of their fathers for their inheritance, which is the land of Jerusalem, which is the promised land unto them forever, saith the Father.
>
> 30 And it shall come to pass that the time cometh, when the fulness of my gospel shall be preached unto them;
>
> 31 And they shall believe in me, that I am Jesus Christ, the Son of God, and shall pray unto the Father in my name.
>
> 3 Nephi 20:29–31

New and Everlasting Covenant

All covenants and ordinances of the gospel of Jesus Christ are collectively known as the New and Everlasting covenant. There are many names for specific covenants in scripture. We may be familiar with "Abrahamic covenant" or "baptismal covenant." There are even references to "a" new and everlasting covenant of marriage. When the Lord makes a covenant with us, it is all part of the new and everlasting covenant. The Lord spoke to Joseph Smith, telling him that He was speaking again to humanity so, "That mine everlasting covenant might be established" (D&C 1:22). Stated simply, "This covenant, often referred to as the 'new and everlasting covenant,' encompasses the fulness of the gospel of Jesus Christ, including all ordinances and covenants necessary for the salvation of humanity" (D&C 66:2).*

After the Lord binds Himself to us in covenant, our task has just begun. The Savior then takes us in and carefully works at teaching and training us how to become like Him. We walk the covenant path, learning to follow Him. We must have faith, repent, have received ordinances, and endure to the end (2 Peter 2:20–22). In the temple, we make additional covenants and receive beautiful blessings from the Lord. Learning to be a disciple of Christ is following Him in all we do. These are the promises we make when we make covenants. We covenant to love Him, follow Him, and do all He asks of us.

The Story of the Golden Calf

One of my favorite ways to understand what a covenant means is seen in the story of the golden calf in the book of Exodus. It is easy to understand what a covenant *is*. It is not difficult to know the terms and promises we make when studying a covenant. The beauty and power of a covenant are not the technical aspects but the meaning. That's when it is helpful to look at a real example. And when we read the story of the golden calf, it might not jump out at us that this is an example of a covenant relationship. But I think you'll see that is precisely what the Lord wants us to remember. It is profound and

* Marcus B. Nash, "The New and Everlasting Covenant," *Liahona*, December 2015.

beautiful in what it tells us about the ferocity of the Lord's love and commitment to us.

The story of the golden calf starts in the Old Testament. Let's return to the story of Moses, Aaron, and the Israelites, in the book of Exodus.

Moses and the Exodus

The Israelites have grown numerous in Egypt. The Pharaoh does not remember Joseph, who saved Egypt and Israel from famine (see Genesis 27–50). The Israelites, once a family, have been blessed, just as the Lord promised Abraham, Isaac, and Jacob. This blessing threatens Pharaoh, the King of Egypt. He tries to work them into submission. Then, when that didn't work, he committed a quiet genocide, plotting for the death of the baby boys, the sons of Israel (see Exodus 1).

It is now we meet one of our famous deliverers, Moses. Hidden by his mother at birth, Moses' mother Jochebed can no longer hide a three-month-old. She makes a tiny ark, places her precious son inside, and sets him adrift down the Nile. Baby Moses' sister, Miriam, watches over the boy as he travels down the river. Then, a miracle happens! The daughter of Pharaoh finds the baby and adopts him as her own. Miriam cleverly offers her mother as a nursemaid (Exodus 2). Moses is saved!

Moses grows up in Pharaoh's house but eventually kills an Egyptian in defense of one of his people and flees. He hides in Midian where, giving up his Egyptian life, he becomes a shepherd and meets his wife, Zipporah. During this crucial part of his life, he is called as a prophet and meets God face to face (see Exodus 2–3, Moses 1–2). God tells Moses His goal in sending Moses to free the Israelites. Moses's mission isn't what you'd guess. It is not solely to free them from bondage. It isn't to spite Pharoah for killing the baby boys. The Lord tells Moses that He wants to free the Israelites, His covenant people, to *meet with them*. The Lord wants to bring them to that place where Moses talks to the Lord and speaks to his covenant children, just like He is doing with Moses.

> 6 I am the God of thy father, the God of Abraham, the God of Isaac, and the God of Jacob. And Moses hid his face; for he was afraid to look upon God.
>
> 7 And the Lord said, I have surely seen the affliction of
> my people which are in Egypt, and have heard their cry
> by reason of their taskmasters; for I know their sorrows;
> 8 And I am come down to deliver them out of the hand of
> the Egyptians, and to bring them up out of that land unto
> a good land and a large, unto a land flowing with milk
> and honey. . . . 10 Come now therefore, and I will send thee
> unto Pharaoh, that thou mayest bring forth my people the
> children of Israel out of Egypt.
>
> 11 And Moses said unto God, Who am I, that I should go unto Pharaoh, and that I should bring forth the children of Israel out of Egypt?
>
> 12 And he said, Certainly *I will be with thee*; and this shall be a token unto thee, that I have sent thee: When thou hast brought forth the people out of Egypt, ye shall serve God upon this mountain.
>
> Exodus 3:6–8, 10–12, emphasis added

The Lord promises Moses that He will be with him. And the proof that all of this is divinely directed will be that the people will return and worship upon this mountain!

So far in the Exodus story, we have a few key elements we should remember. First, this story is a continuation of the family of Abraham. We are reminded of Joseph, the part of the book of Genesis, and the history that just ended. We tend to skip over that part, but Exodus starts that way to tie in the book of Genesis. We are reminded of the Lord's promises to Abraham, Isaac, Jacob, and Joseph.

Then, we highlight that God is involved in saving the Israelites, even when it seems all is lost. In their case, the Egyptian Pharoah tries to oppress them and kill them. This is a story about the Lord saving His people. He hears their cries, feels their sorrows and despair, and steps in to offer them salvation.

Next, we learn about the role of a prophet, meeting God on a high mountain. And there, we understand God's purpose, *to invite all the people to meet Him* on that very same mountain. The Lord called a prophet to call us into a special relationship with Him.

Mountains, Gardens, Altars, Rest

One technique scripture uses to teach an important concept is the use of a motif. A motif is a symbolic image or idea that frequently appears in a story. It is used to accentuate a pattern in the story helps us understand a big concept. Motifs are often images or elements that repeat and teach us about a bigger idea or theme. I think of a motif like a hyperlink. When you are on a webpage or an app, a hyperlink is a button that links you to a related page. A hyperlink is often underlined and colored blue so that you know it is connecting to another idea.

Mountains, gardens, altars, and rest are all motifs in scripture. Each site is described repeatedly in scripture to teach us vital concepts about spiritual realities. They are both physical and symbolic locations that are repeatedly used to teach us essential concepts about spiritual truths.

Let's take a minute and talk about an important place that is commonly talked about in scripture, the temple.

Wait a minute! The header says, "Mountain, Gardens, Altars, Rest!" you say. What does a temple have to do with these things? They all refer to a living with and like our Father. They all refer to the same idea—exaltation.

In the beginning . . . we know how this story goes. God creates the Heavens and the Earth. All of creation is a temple for the Lord. He says in Isaiah 66:1, "Heaven is my throne, and the earth is my footstool: where is the house that ye build unto me? And what is the place of my rest?" This connection then ties us to the idea that the "temple is a microcosm of creation."*

* D. A. Neal and John Anthony Dunne, "Eden, Garden of," ed. John D. Barry et al., *The Lexham Bible Dictionary* (Bellingham, WA: Lexham Press, 2016), 123.

Mountain imagery is frequent. Meeting or receiving laws and revelation from God is frequently done on a mountain (Acts 7:38, 53; Galatians 3:19; Hebrews 2:2; Deuteronomy 33:2; Exodus 24:9–11; Isaiah 33:20; Psalms 26:8, 74:7; 1 Chronicles 9:23). Nephi experiences a vision, "caught away in the Spirit of the Lord, yea, into an exceedingly high mountain" (1 Nephi 11:1). He is later commanded to go to a mountain to converse with the Lord again (1 Nephi 17:7). The brother of Jared speaks with the Lord on a mountain (Ether 3:1–4:1), and the Urim and Thummim is given to him on a mountain (D&C 17:1). Moses is "caught up into a mountain" to speak to the Lord (Moses 1:1, 42). This is just a small list of examples! God frequently uses mountains as a place to meet and talk to people.

The mountain and the temple are both places where the Lord meets us, and also they are places of learning and worship. An altar is where this worship occurs. The altar is the place where we sacrifice, in the similitude of the sacrifice of Jesus Christ.

> [6] And after many days an angel of the Lord appeared unto
> Adam, saying:
> Why dost thou offer sacrifices unto the Lord?
> And Adam said unto him: I know not, save the Lord
> commanded me.
>
> [7] And then the angel spake, saying:
> This thing is a similitude of the sacrifice of the Only
> Begotten of the Father, which is full of grace and truth.
> [8] Wherefore, thou shalt do all that thou doest in the name
> of the Son, and thou shalt repent and call upon God in the
> name of the Son forevermore.
>
> [9] And in that day the Holy Ghost fell upon Adam, which
> beareth record of the Father and the Son, saying:
> I am the Only Begotten of the Father from the
> beginning, henceforth and forever, that as thou hast fallen
> thou mayest be redeemed, and all mankind, even as many as
> will.

> [10] And in that day Adam blessed God and was filled, and began to prophesy concerning all the families of the earth, saying:
>
> Blessed be the name of God, for because of my transgression my eyes are opened, and in this life I shall have joy, and again in the flesh I shall see God.
>
> Moses 5:6–10

Mountains, gardens, altars, and temples are locations and images that are often connected with meeting God. It is there that we are welcomed into His presence. We worship, are taught, and make sacred covenants in a holy place. We are in communion, a relationship, with Him as we are invited into His Home. Another way of describing this transcendent experience is "entering into His rest." Alma speaks of the important role of those who hold the priesthood to help others enter into the Lord's rest.

> [2] And those priests were ordained after the order of his Son, in a manner that thereby the people might know in what manner to look forward to his Son for redemption. . . .
>
> [6] And thus being called by this holy calling, and ordained unto the high priesthood of the holy order of God, to teach his commandments unto the children of men, that they also might enter into his rest.
>
> Alma 13:2, 6

Through the power of the priesthood, the Lord invites us into His presence. There we learn of the plan of salvation. We are to help teach these things to the rest of our human family so that all can have the blessing of salvation. All of this is "entering into His rest."

Returning to the Lord's Presence

The common idea is that God wants to have us return to Him. We often say, "return to His presence" or "entering into His rest." The idea is simple but is said to be in many different ways. John the Baptist reminded us "the kingdom of heaven is at hand" (Matthew 3:1–2). He was telling us that we could regain God's presence through Him. We could return to Eden. We could go home.

So, while we say "return to" we are progressing. "Entering the Lord's rest" is not going *backward* but *forwards*. In reality, we are progressing and returning to His Presence, the celestial realm, the celestial kingdom. It is easier to sum up the idea by saying "return to Him" or "return to His presence" even though we mean "progress and enter into exaltation."

The Promised Land

Before we look at the story of the golden calf, there is one more key idea about covenants I want to explore. We often hear about covenants and an idea of a promised land. How does that all fit in with this temple/garden/altar/rest idea?

If our goal is to return to Eden, we might ask, "Where are we really returning to?" It is easy to say, "heaven" or "the celestial kingdom." Yes, I think that is right. Also, one of the promises of the Abrahamic covenant is the promise of a place. The promised land becomes an ideal and an actuality. In Genesis 17:8, there is a promise of land, "and I will give unto thee, and to thy seed after thee, the land wherein thou art a stranger, all the land of Canaan, for an everlasting possession; and I will be their God" (see also Abraham 2:6–11).

Interestingly, Nephi and his family are promised a land as well. "Notwithstanding our afflictions, we have obtained a land of promise, a land which is choice above all other lands; a land which the Lord God hath covenanted with me should be a land for the inheritance of my seed" (2 Nephi 1:5). Lehi was told, as part of his covenant promises that he and his family had a blessing related to land. They were told, "inasmuch as thy seed shall keep my commandments, they shall prosper in the land of promise" (1 Nephi 4:14; see also 2:20).

When the Lord returns, He will return to rule over a "new heaven and a new earth" (Revelation 21:1). The Doctrine and Covenants explain that the sea of glass in Revelation 4:6 "is the earth, in its sanctified, immortal, and eternal state" (D&C 77:1). We also learn that will be our eternal inheritance (D&C 63:20–21).

Where does that leave us? We see that we are reminded of an Eden, a promised land, where we can live with and like the Lord. The Lord promises us a glorified Eden, a "new heaven and a new earth." As we read through scripture, we are going to see this theme repeated over and over. It might be a different word, a different example, but it all points to the same idea—inheriting celestial glory and living a life with and like our Father in Heaven.

It's just a lot simpler to say, "promised land."

The Golden Calf

Let's return to the story of Moses, the Exodus, and the golden calf. Recalling our setup, we learned of Moses and his miraculous beginnings. Then, we learn of Moses meeting the Lord on the mountain and the Lord's invitation to all of Israel. God wants to invite all of them to meet Him on the very same mountain. Now, we have set the stage of the mountain-garden-temple-rest motif, and we resume the story. We want to understand the spiritual and emotional meaning of the covenant. We want to really grasp this idea of the Lord's covenantal love.

After Moses has led the Israelites out of servitude in Egypt, they worship an idol. This event might not be so shocking if we had not just made a promise to "not make . . . any graven image" (Exodus 20:4). One of the first of the Ten Commandments they just promised to keep they are already breaking. On top of that, they had just witnessed miracles! The people had seen the wonders of the Lord as plagues from God. They saw Moses' staff turn to a serpent. They witnessed the Passover when their firstborn sons were passed over and saved by the Lord. They escaped Egypt and crossed the sea on dry ground. They traveled to a holy mountain. They saw lightning, heard thunder, and witnessed the fire of the Lord's presence.

God had rescued them! He wanted to welcome them into His presence and meet them on the holy mountain. Before they ascend, Moses goes up to receive the law—the covenant rules to which they have agreed. While Moses is up on the mountain, they begin to doubt, fear, and falter.

> And when the people saw that Moses delayed to come down out of the mount, the people gathered themselves together unto Aaron, and said unto him, Up, make us gods, which shall go before us; for as for this Moses, the man that brought us up out of the land of Egypt, we wot not what is become of him.
>
> Exodus 32:1

Moses has been up there for a long time. They start to worry. Their relationship with the Lord is new and recent, and they're still learning how to be in covenant with Him. Moses gets word of what's going on below and descends the mountain. The Lord is understandably upset. Moses intercedes, acting as in similitude of our Lord, and saves the people. Moses knows that the Lord with be faithful to the promises He made in covenant to Abraham and all of Abraham's family. The Lord is merciful, recalling His covenant with the people (Exodus 32:1–14).

How can the people, with so many promises, who have witnessed so many miracles, already be forgetting? How could they sin like this, break the covenants they made just days ago? It is easy to think of the Israelites as foolish or "not like us." But their story is our story. How often do we sin, make mistakes, backslide, or forget our covenants shortly after making them? We are probably more like the Israelites than we care to admit. The good news is that the golden calf's story is not over. The point of the story is not their sin and repentance. The point of the story is what happens next!

It is at this point that the Lord reveals something about Himself. And this is key—the Lord is telling us what *He is like.* He shares his characteristics, nature, traits, and His character.

> [6] And the Lord passed by before him, and proclaimed, The Lord, The Lord God, merciful and gracious, longsuffering, and abundant in goodness and truth, [7] Keeping mercy for thousands, forgiving iniquity and transgression and sin.
>
> Exodus 34:6–7

One of the most quoted verses within the Bible is Exodus 34:6–7. Prophets repeat this scripture over and over again within the pages of scripture. He is merciful. He is gracious. He is full of "grace and truth." They want us to know this about the Lord.

In this verse, the Lord describes Himself. He tells us He is merciful. He is full of grace. He is also very patient. His love is so great that He will love our families and us forever. He is committed to us despite our failings, doubts, or sin. He is absolutely dedicated to us, forever. He has bound Himself to us in covenant love. He is our God. When we fail, sin, make mistakes, drift away, rebel, or make "golden calves," He will remember His covenant promises. He will be merciful.

I Am a Jealous God

"For I the Lord thy God am a jealous God" (Exodus 20:5). In the Ten Commandments, we hear an odd phrase. "Jealous God" sounds strange to us. We think of jealousy as a negative emotion and one that we should avoid. Describing the Lord as jealous is a little unsettling to our modern ears. Unfortunately, we haven't updated this word in our English scriptures. In English, the word jealous has shifted meaning over the centuries, so we are left confused.

What does "jealous" really mean here? God loves us so profoundly, with such intensity that it is difficult to describe. Jealousy here isn't the insecure human jealousy. Instead, in scripture it is covenant love. It is sincere devotion. It is love like a husband has for a wife, whom he has covenanted to love and protect. It is the love a wife has for a husband, for whom she will support and be devoted. In a word, God is utterly faithful. A better way to say it would be "full of covenant love and devotion." Moses reminds the house of Israel about God's utter devotion as they enter the promised land "Be strong and courageous. Do not fear or be in dread of them, for it is the Lord your God who goes with you. He will not leave you or forsake you" (Deuteronomy 31:6, ESV).

This is what it *means* to be in a covenant with the Lord. He will love and help us, no matter how often or much we fail. He is faithful. He forgives. Being in a covenant with the Lord of all creation reminds us that He has already promised to forgive. He has already told us He will welcome us into His arms. He is full of covenant love.

Becoming like He Is

I love this testimony of the Lord. He is loving and binds Himself to us. He also asks us to be like Him. And this is where the gathering of Israel becomes so essential. It isn't enough that we know Him. He asks us to be like Him. He loves us so very much; He is willing to share everything He has. He wants to share His love, His blessings, and the opportunity to be like Him. He shares Himself. "Thine ears shall hear a word behind thee, saying, This is the way, walk ye in it" (Isaiah 30:21).

Key Ideas to Remember

- Covenants are promises the Lord makes with us.
- A covenant is a promise of a relationship with the Savior.
- "We love Him, because He first loved us."
- We are often required to do specific things in order to qualify for covenant blessings. Becoming a true disciple can fill us with such love that obedience is no longer an obligation but something that pours out of us.
- While there are many covenants, they can all be called the new and everlasting covenant.
- The Lord uses repeating motifs to teach us about living with Him: mountains, gardens, altars, temples, rest.
- The golden calf story highlights the Lord's true nature: patient, loving, and full of covenant love.
- Being in a covenant with the Lord means He has already promised to welcome us back.
- The Lord's description of Himself is that He is merciful and full of covenant love toward us.

PART 2:

SCATTERING *and* EXILE

The Twins

Gloria wanted to keep the twins. Having a baby, let alone two babies was not in her plans. To be honest, she didn't really have any plans—at least not yet. Life had been hard, really hard. Growing up only speaking Spanish, then being thrown into school at age seven with kids who didn't understand her had made her different. She had worked hard to fit in, to make friends.

After her father died—before even—she was on her own. She was on her own again now. But this time, she had twin babies. She wanted to give it a try. She wanted to be a good mother.

She had been visiting the twins, supervised by a social worker, one hour at a time. She could set up a time to visit the twins at their current foster home. The foster family was different nearly every time she visited. Twins were particularly hard to care for and a challenge most foster families struggled to handle. As a result, the twins cried a lot. They refused to be separated from each other, even as tiny babies.

During one visit, Gloria held the girls. The babies were so small and so tiny. Gloria thought, "We could be a family. It would just be us girls." She decided to take them home. She called the State Agency and let them know she would take the twins.

Gloria took the twins home. She was still at her sister Carol's apartment, and now, they had just doubled the population. The twins required her every attention. She gave them bottles, changed them, talked to them. She even went to the store and picked up a few items. Getting them bundled up and everyone out the door took most of the morning. Walking the twins to the corner store was a major event. When she got back, with a small bag of items, she realized how many, many things babies would need. They would need everything, *and how would she do it?*

Gloria was angry, sad, and frustrated. Why wasn't there a way to make this work? Sadly, she realized that even though she might be able to love the twins, she couldn't provide everything they needed. That night she talked to her sister, Carol. She told Carol she didn't think that staying with her was the best for the girls. Carol had been expecting the news. Frankly, Carol had been trying to figure out a way to support her young sister and the twins herself. She also realized that the greatest gift they could give was to let them go.

Gloria had spent just a day with the twins, and she knew. Seeing the two little ones there, in the apartment, it all became very obvious what she must do. She must love them enough to let them go. Eventually, she picked up the phone. She called the adoption agency and told them the news. The babies were going to their new home.

Chapter 5

SPREADING OUT

As we return to this theme of a remnant, a pattern emerges. The Lord has saved a portion, a scrap, a family, or an individual from the beginning. Amid evil, destruction, or conflict, He delivers a remnant. This remnant, or the ones left, is also a reason to hope to restore the whole. The Lord will save a remnant like Noah on an ark, or the Nephites from Jerusalem, or babies in an adoption.

When we talk of the gathering of Israel, it is always the second part of the story. To gather something implies it must be scattered. We tend to get right to the good part, the gathering. We jump over the sad part. Studying the scattering is the sad part of the story. We don't want to dwell on that, do we? However, the gathering, the Lord's love and plan to save us, is more meaningful when we understand how far He will go to gather us in.

The scattering is both a historical event and a theological concept. Scripture will show us real-world examples and encourage us to see the ideas and themes presented. In those concepts, the themes, we may see the scattering happen in our own lives.

There are historical examples. We recall the Jaredites were led to a new home (Ether 1). We also remember the Lehites were saved from the destruction of Jerusalem by being scattered to a new land. We will also see the loss of an entire nation, like the scattering of the ten tribes of Israel. (We'll cover this one specifically in just a few minutes.) Over and over again, we will see humanity scattered, driven, exiled, and lost.

There are spiritual scatterings, too. Isaiah describes this spiritual scattering as the Lord hiding His face: "But your iniquities have separated between you and your God, and your sins have hid his face from you, that he will not hear" (Isaiah 59:2).

Let's unpack the ideas behind the scattering.

Eden: Zooming In

To understand the theme and ideas of the scattering, we should go back to our zoomed-out view, Genesis 1–11. We will learn the ideas that will reverberate and ripple out through all of scripture. In the early parts of Genesis, we will see this idea at least twice.

In Eden, we first see the idea of being scattered. Recalling the story once again . . .

Adam and Eve are given a beautiful garden in which to live. There they walk and talk with God. They are given commandments to have children and take care of the garden. They are also told not to partake of the fruit of the tree of knowledge of good and evil. They are deceived, partake, and as a result will die. The Lord is not surprised but has a plan for their return. The humans covenant with the Lord to obey Him, and a Savior is provided so that they may return. They are then exiled from the garden (Genesis 1–3, Abraham 3–5, Moses 2–5). In this brief overview, we recall a few key elements:

- God means for us to live in a beautiful home.
- Through our disobedience we are separated from Him physically and spiritually.
- We are exiled, scattered, and separated through sin and the effects of a fallen world.
- The Savior is provides a way to return.
- The Lord offers covenants for us to learn and grow. He binds Himself to us in love and faithfulness, promising never to leave us.

Leaving Eden is our first scattering. In our exile from the presence of the Lord, we are separated and scattered. The story of Adam and Eve isn't just their story. We remember it is our story, too.

There is another story of exile and scattering in the early parts of Genesis. After the expulsion from the Garden of Eden, we find another "big picture" view. After the story of Noah, we see humanity has once again flourished. The people have become numerous and also wicked. The majority turn from God and decide to try and choose good and evil for themselves. They choose to create their own way to return to Eden, to our heavenly home. They build a great tower, and they name it Babylon.

Babel and Babylon

Just a little context here. In Genesis, they call this city Babel, but we use the name Babylon in all the other translations of the word. The city is Babylon, which in Hebrew is a wordplay on *balal*. *Balal* means to mix or mingle, confound.* So if we read the phrase about the confounding of the languages, it would sound like this:

> 7 Go to, let us go down, and there confound their language,
> that they may not understand one another's speech. 8 So the
> Lord scattered them abroad from thence upon the face of all
> the earth: and they left off to build the city.
>
> 9 Therefore is the name of it called Babel; because the Lord
> did there confound the language of all the earth: and from
> thence did the Lord scatter them abroad upon the face of all
> the earth.
>
> Genesis 11:7–9

Translators have left the Hebrew name of the city, Babel, to underscore that the people were confounded, confused, and scattered. The name of the city as Babel reminds of the idea. We cannot confound the Lord's purposes but instead will be confounded. It is nice that in English, the words work, too. They babbled or were confused in Babel. Get it? Hebrew authors are so clever and appreciate a good pun.

The other 249 times the city is named in the Old Testament, it is called Babylon. Similarly, in the New Testament, Book of Mormon,

* Brown, S. Driver, and C. Briggs, *The Brown-Driver-Briggs Hebrew and English Lexicon* (Boston: Hendrickson Publishers, 2004), 215 and 2022. See also entry 1101.

and Doctrine and Covenants, any time the Lord wants to use the idea of the sinful city, it is called Babylon instead of Babel. But it is the same place. Babylon becomes the city of exile. It is also a symbolic city representing the scattering. Babylon becomes the great city, the first major city in scripture, and it is set up in opposition to Zion, God's city.

Zion

We have an opposition city to help us see the differences between living the Lord's way or the world's way. If Babylon is the city representing the world, what is God's city?

> 17 The fear of the Lord was upon all nations, so great was the
> glory of the Lord, which was upon his people. And the Lord
> blessed the land, and they were blessed upon the mountains,
> and upon the high places, and did flourish. 18 And the Lord
> called his people Zion, because they were of one heart and
> one mind, and dwelt in righteousness; and there was no poor
> among them.
>
> Moses 7:17–18.

Zion reminds us of Eden, a place full of the Lord's blessing. In Eden, we flourish, become the best humanity we can be, and live in love and peace. Zion is an actual location and a symbolic representation. We'll return to this idea of Eden and Zion, where we return to God's presence. For now, let's continue exploring this idea of scattering.

Babylon then becomes a symbol and an actual city, in contrast to Zion. Living in exile, being scattered is living in Babylon. In the Old Testament, the great scattering is done by the nation of Babylon. The Tower of Babel is the zoomed-out view. We get our central idea and theme. Scripture has another zoomed-in perspective to reinforce the concept. When we think of the scattering, there is one example we think of more than any other. And that is the breaking of the tribes.

The Scattering Seems Harsh

Every four years, as we start our study of the Old Testament, I hear a common comment. "The Old Testament shows a harsh view of God. I like the Book of Mormon or New Testament with the loving side of the Savior." It hurts my heart that we only see the story of the Old Testament as one of rebuke. I get it, though. The Old Testament has many stories of sin, separation, and challenges. However, we see many stories of a loving God working to redeem humanity. Why the disconnect? This idea that the Old Testament has a harsh view of God may be because of the perspective.

Old Testament as a Flashback

The majority of the Old Testament is told as a response to the question, "If we were the chosen people of the Lord, how did we get here?"

When we read the story of the Old Testament, it is often a flashback. The editors, authors, and prophets selected stories to explain the mission of the Savior. They also showed their people, now living after their people had been overtaken and carried into exile, explaining how it happened. Thus, most Old Testament books are prophets warning the people what will happen or explaining why something did. It is all a kind of flashback. We get warning after warning of what will happen if we, the people of Israel, don't turn back to the Lord. Or, it is a retrospective, showing the house of Israel what they had and why, despite being in covenant with God, they found themselves outside the promised land. One of the most defining and critical events in the history of the house of Israel was the exile. To help understand the importance of the gathering of Israel, we will refer to the exile as "the scattering."

The Promise of a King and Kingdom

God promised Abraham many significant blessings. One of these is a place, a land. This blessing is a crucial component of the Abrahamic covenant. (Reminder—I may say new and everlasting covenant or Abrahamic covenant, but I mean the same thing, as we already

*Image of the divided kingdom, including capital cities of Samaria and Jerusalem about the time of books of Kings.**

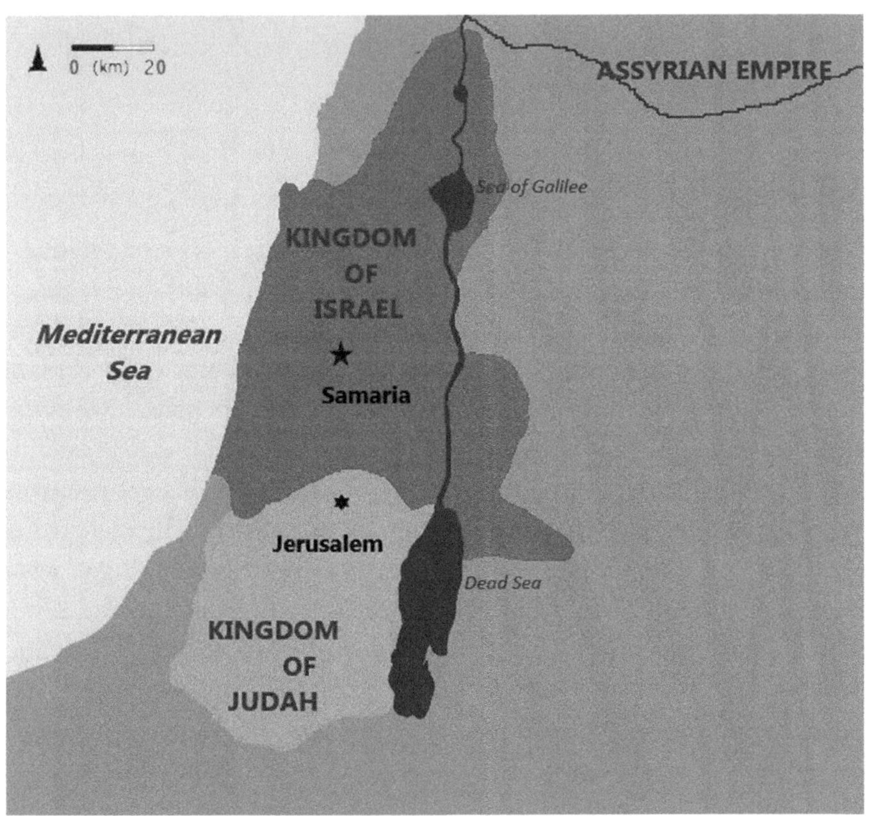

* Image redrawn by Lori L. Denning; original image found at https://en.wikipedia.org/wiki/Kingdom_of_Israel_(Samaria)#/media/File:Kingdoms_of_Israel_and_Judah_map_830.svg.

discussed). For the people of the Old Testament, they looked to the land of Canaan to settle and be a place of prosperity for them.

In addition to a place to settle down and raise families, the Israelites also wanted a king. They wanted someone to rule and protect them. Samuel, the prophet, had put a judge in charge, but the people wanted something else. The Elders of Israel come to Samuel, "And said unto him, Behold, thou art old, and thy sons walk not in thy ways: now make us a king to judge us like all the nations" (1 Samuel 8:5).

God promised Israel a benevolent and just ruler. 2 Samuel 7 recounts the promise to the House of David. "I will set up thy seed after thee, which shall proceed out of thy bowels, and I will establish his kingdom" (2 Samuel 7:12). And again, "And thine house and thy kingdom shall be established for ever before thee: thy throne shall be established for ever" (2 Samuel 7:16).

Under Saul then David, the Kingdom of Israel, a united kingdom, is finally established. All the tribes of Israel are finally united in one entity. David creates the capital as Jerusalem. His son, Solomon, builds the temple there. Are David and Solomon the answer to the promised king? Will they finally usher in peace, justice, and the Lord's holy reign? Sadly, the united kingdom only lasts a generation or so. Tyranny and oppression from within drive the kingdom apart. The tribes split, separating into two parts. With ten tribes in the North, they are collectively known as Israel. The two tribes in the South are called by the name Judah.

Both kingdoms Israel and Judah struggle to be faithful to their covenants. The books of Kings catalog these events, telling of the separation of the kingdoms and the ministry of the prophet Elijah. The prophet Elijah has a major role in the gathering, and we'll return to him shortly. For now, remember that he lived in a time when the people, including their leaders, had strayed from the covenant.

The Lord promised Israel great blessings. Blessings of prosperity, a place to put it, prosperity, priesthood, and more. The land of Canaan was promised to Abraham (Genesis 13:15, 17:8). After the Exodus, fleeing Egypt, the Israelites are given specific portions of the land with their tribe (Numbers 34:1–12). An essential component of this blessing is the requirement of covenant faithfulness. King Solomon, David's son, is told that the land will be taken from him when he fails to keep his covenants. Solomon had married outside the covenant and turned to false worship: "Wherefore the Lord said unto Solomon, Forasmuch as this is done of thee, and thou hast not kept my covenant and my statutes, which I have commanded thee, I will surely rend the kingdom from thee, and will give it to thy servant" (1 Kings 11:11).

Just as Solomon failed to keep his covenants and oppressed the people, the rulers who followed him failed. Solomon's son, Rehoboam, does not bring peace rather more insults (1 Kings 12). The Northern Kingdom splits apart from the South. Now there is a divided kingdom, Israel, and Judah. The books of Kings continue in this manner, mainly cataloging the kings' failures to keep their covenants. One after another, the kings of the North or the South fail to keep their covenants, turning to the worship of false gods and introducing sin.

If the books of Kings had a scoreboard, the Northern and Southern Kingdoms would lose. According to scripture, the Northern Kings fail utterly. No Kings are successful in following the Lord. The Southern Kings do only slightly better with only two Kings at worshipping God. The kings of both kingdoms lead the people astray, forget the Lord, and worship other gods (see 1 and 2 Kings). In short, they do a terrible job staying faithful to their covenant.

As a result the people are overrun and sent into exile.

Kingdom of Israel

In the North part of the promised land is the Kingdom of Israel. It is ruled by its capital city, Samaria. The Southern Kingdom is called Judah. Its capital is Jerusalem. The tricky part of all of this geography and series of kingdoms is that sometimes they are referred to by the kingdom name, Israel or Judah. Yet, other times, they are called Samaria or Jerusalem by the capital cities. Yet they'll be referenced by the chief tribes, Ephraim or Judah, more often than not. Additionally, some prophets taught to only Israel or Judah and not both. Sometimes, the tribes were already lost when a prophet was around. The timelines are often garbled based on where the books are in order in the Old Testament. And still, to make it even more confusing, there are times when the names, capitals, and people are mixed. The conversation might call one by the tribe, the other by the capital. A chart can make this easier to follow:

	Northern Kingdom	Southern Kingdom
Called	Kingdom of Israel	Kingdom of Judah
Dominant Tribe	Ephraim	Judah
Capital	Shiloh, Samaria	Jerusalem, Judah
Count of the tribes*	10	2
Location	Northern part of Canaan	Southern part of Caanan
Key prophets	Elijah, Elisha, Amos, Hosea	Isaiah, Micah, Joel, Jeremiah, Lehi
Overrun date (approximation)	720 BCE	586 BCE
Conquering superpower	Asssyrians	Babylonians
*All tribes are to be found, including Levi, in both Northern and Southern Kingdoms. Generally, however, the land allotment given to the tribes of Israel follows this designation.		

What happens next is the scattering of Israel. Because the Kingdom of Israel does not keep its covenants, the Lord's protection is withdrawn. Prophet after prophet comes to warn the people and leaders to return and repent. The Northern Kingdom does not listen from Elijah to Elisha, from Amos to Hosea. Eventually, the superpower of the day, Assyria, conquers the Kingdom of Israel, takes the people into captivity, and the tribes into exile (1 Chronicles 5:26, 2 Kings 15:29, 2 Kings 17:3–6). The northern tribes, including Ephraim and Manasseh, are carried into exile and "lost" (2 Kings 18:11–12).

Kingdom of Judah

While the Kingdom of Israel is now scattered, the Southern Kingdom continues for a few hundred more years. Now called Judah, the remnants of the tribes of Israel continue, with slightly more success than their Northern neighbors at keeping their covenants. However, they fail despite prophetic warnings from Isaiah, Lehi, Joel, Jeremiah, Zephaniah, Micah, and others. The Assyrians are no longer the ruling civilization but the Babylonians (also called the neo-Babylonians, to distinguish them from the ancient group we find in Genesis).* The Kingdom of Judah is also scattered, the temple destroyed, and the people carried away to Babylon. It is here we read of prophets in exile like Daniel and Ezekiel. Also, this time when Judah was carried into Babylon is sometimes called the Exile.

The books of Daniel and Ezekiel, and parts of Jeremiah, teach us how to live in the world but not of it. We will live our lives outside of Eden. In the world, we must learn how to rely on God, listen to His prophets, and be guided by the Holy Spirit. Despite these moments of respite, we long to return to the promised land. We want to return to Eden.

But what about the Kingdom of Judah historically? Will they remain in Babylon? Will the temple be destroyed forever? When will the true King come to save and lead His people?

Return, or Was It?

After all of this destruction, both Northern and Southern Kingdoms were sacked. The temple in Jerusalem has been destroyed. The people have been carried away into exile and servitude. Lehi and his family have been carried away as a remnant. Is this where the story ends for the family of Israel?

Not exactly.

Not too long after the Babylonian captivity began, the Babylonian empire fell (2 Kgs 24:1–25:22; 2 Chronicles 36:6–13; Ezra 5:12–6:5; Nehemiah 7:6; Jeremiah 21:2–52:28; Ezekiel 33:21). But it isn't exactly good news for the Kingdom of Judah. Regime after regime conquers the people.† After Babylon come the Persians, after the Persians, the Greeks, then the Romans. That isn't even a definitive list. There are even more kingdoms that rule and oppress Judah. Eventually, however, they are allowed to return. And some do (see the books of Ezra

---

* Luigi Caiafa, "Mesopotamia, Archaeology Of, Middle Bronze through Iron Age," ed. John D. Barry et al., *The Lexham Bible Dictionary* (Bellingham, WA: Lexham Press, 2016).

† Caiafa.

and Nehemiah). Judah, now called "the Jews" by their Greek-speaking neighbors, is still being ruled by others.

It isn't just the tyranny of other rulers that causes the Jews to suffer. They struggle to follow the Lord, keep his commandments, and remember their covenants. While they have regained the land, they have not reclaimed its rule. And while they have rebuilt the temple, they have not regained the presence of the Lord.

Scattering Continues

Eventually, a remnant from the Kingdom of Judah is allowed to leave Babylon and return to Jerusalem (Ezra 1:1–4). And some do! The story is told in the books of Ezra and Nehemiah. While some from Judah return to rebuild the nation, surprisingly, many choose to stay in Babylon. Those that remain in Babylon have mixed results. Some follow the Lord, while others become like the people around them. They have learned to be like Babylon, embracing all the cultures and beliefs. The Kingdom of Judah, although back in the promised land, has become spiritually lost. The Exiles were home, returned to the promised land, yet they were still oppressed. The Northern Kingdoms were still lost, and the Southern was still occupied.

They are lost in place.

Babylon becomes a symbol of the world. While it was an actual city, we see that Babylon is much more. It becomes a symbol of our spiritual separation from the divine ideal. Babylon lives in each of us. Like the ancient family of Israel, we all will have times when we fail. We will sin and fall short.

In some cases, we outright will rebel. We will knowingly choose evil. And like Babylon, we will cause harm to ourselves and others. We allow Babylon to live in our hearts. Babylon, being scattered, is something more universal.

We Are all Scattered

The scattering is more than just a historical event. It is a universal condition. Like Israel, there are times when we will be in emotional or spiritual exile. We will be separated from the Lord. The causes of separation from Him can be of our own doing or from the poor choices of others. Our exile may also be the fallen nature of our world. No matter the cause, we will all be a part of a scattering. Just as we see in the pattern from the exile from Eden, from Israel, our home, is something we will all feel. We will all be scattered, exiled, and separated from God.

The great prophet Nephi, son of Lehi, writes of this spiritual separation in a psalm. We are not alone in feeling scattered, alone, and separated from Him. Nephi writes,

> O wretched man that I am!
> Yea, my heart sorroweth because of my flesh;
> my soul grieveth because of mine iniquities.
> I am encompassed about,
> because of the temptations
> and sins which do so easily best me.
> And when I desire to rejoice,
> my heart groaneth because of my sins;
>
> Nevertheless, I know in who I have trusted.
> My God had been my support;
> he hath led me through mine afflictions in the wilderness;
> and he hath preserved me upon the waters of the great deep.
> He hath filled me with his love,
> even unto the consuming of my flesh.
> He hath confounded mine enemies,
> unto the causing of them to quake before me.
>
> Behold, he hath heard my cry by day,
> and he hath given me knowledge by visions in the night-time.
> And by day have I waxed bold in mighty prayer before him;
> yea, my voice have I sent up on high;
> and angels came down and ministered unto me.
>
> And upon the wings of his Spirit
> hath my body been carried away upon exceedingly high mountains.

And mine eyes have beheld great things,
yea, even too great for man;

And why should I yield to sin, because of my flesh?
Yea, why should I give way to temptations,
that the evil one have place in my heart
to destroy my peace and afflict my soul?
Why am I angry because of mine enemy?

Awake, my soul!
No longer droop in sin.
Rejoice, O my heart,
and give place no more for the enemy of my soul.

2 Nephi 4: 17–28, formatting added

The Psalm of Nephi is a beautiful lament about spiritual separation. It is also a poem of praise for the love and generosity of the Lord. Nephi decries the internal sufferings of sin. It is remarkable that Nephi, the prophet who is quick to follow the Lord, shows faith in his father's visions, which the Spirit directs and which has moments of separation, sin, and "scattering." It gives all of us hope that even Nephi felt like us sometimes.

While the hope of the return from exile is present in the books of Ezra and Nehemiah, the underlying theme is that something more is required to usher in God's promised blessings. The answer is that the people must change. We must allow the commandments, the law, to change us from the inside out.

A New Heart

Jeremiah, a prophet of the Exile, prophesies the actual time of the Return when the city and people will be restored. "I will put my law within them, and I will write it on their hearts, and I will be their God; and they shall be my people" (Jeremiah 31:33, NRSV). The true return from the scattering is more than outward actions alone but a time when righteousness flows out of us like "a mighty stream" (Amos 5:24).

Another prophet in Exile, Ezekiel, saw this renewal when he said, "It has come! . . . This is the day of which I have spoken"(Ezekiel 39:8, NRSV). The change that God will make and requires is in the hearts of all of us,

> A new heart I will give you, and a new spirit I will put within you; and I will remove from your body the heart of stone and give you a heart of flesh. I will put my spirit within you, and make you follow my statutes and be careful to observe my ordinances. Then you shall live in the land I gave to your ancestors; and you shall be my people and I will be your God.
>
> Ezekiel 36:26–29, NRSV

Thus, the scriptures describe the Lord as a God of covenant faithfulness who desires to bless His people. Covenant obedience is an extension of the change that has already happened inside. In the tremendous culminating promise, the great messianic King will be our true King, our ruler, and our God.

Key Ideas to Remember

- All of us become scattered and lost at times.
- Babel, Babylon, the lost ten tribes, are all examples of scattering.
- The tribes of Israel split into two parts. Ephraim/Israel in the North and Judah in the South.
- In the Exile, the Kingdom of Israel is spiritually and physically lost. The Kingdom of Judah is spiritually lost in place.
- Babylon becomes a symbol of being spiritually lost.
- We all long to be gathered, return from exile, and be restored.
- The Lord instructs us to change our hearts to begin to return to Him.

PART 3:

KNOWING WHO WE ARE *to* *the* LORD

DNA Test

A few years ago, I got a DNA test that showed my ancestry. Perhaps you have seen them? You get a test kit sent to you in the mail, you send back some DNA samples, and a few weeks later you get a chart showing where your ancestry comes from, based on genetics. While you don't carry all the DNA from every genetic relative, it shows what you inherited. It cannot determine every ethnic difference, but it gives clues to your genetic ancestry.

Being adopted, I had only heard some general idea of my ancestry. My adopted family had deep roots in England and Wales. The Dennings have ancestry charts, large books with photos of ancestors, and narratives and journals. I loved these stories of our family. While my adopted family had many details, my birth family information was scarce. My genetic family history was vague, as a closed adoption does not record such information. Discovering any details about my roots was exciting. I was anxious to get the test results.

Being a twin has some unique genetic markers. If you are identical twins, you have the same genetic makeup. Can you imagine being exactly like someone else? My twin, Lisa, and I look a lot alike. However, just looking at twins, you cannot always determine if they are identical and not fraternal. Even if they are the same gender, they may be fraternal. The only definitive way is a DNA test. Lisa had already received her DNA kit. She had sent me some text images of her results. It was cool, but I was more interested in my own.

Would we be identical twins? Would my genetic clues be the same, or maybe a little different than Lisa's? Where would it say we were from? We had heard that our birth mother had Mexican heritage. While the information on our birth parents was scant, we had also heard our birth father was more Scandinavian, being very blond and blue-eyed. Lisa and I are very fair, have greenish eyes, and have blonde-brown hair. We do not have many distinctive features that would be a clue to our ethnic heritage. We could be from almost anywhere.

Finally, I got an email link that my test had a problem. It looked like it had been tampered with, I had already taken a test, or I was a twin. I called the company, and they gave me the news: my test was exactly like someone else in the database, which, unless it was an earlier test of mine, or I was an identical twin, was genetically impossible. Well, I guess that mystery was solved—we were identical twins. You can go ahead a laugh for those of you who know us. We do look alike have the same mannerisms, laugh, and voice. It would not have been a tough guess to say we were identical. Yet, having the DNA information in my hand with a key element about who I was, was gripping.

They soon sent me a link to their database, showing me the details of my genetic heritage. Showing genetic markers from thirteen different regions, I was from, well, everywhere! The graphics popped up with ancestry from Mexico, England, Scandinavia, Spain, even parts of Africa, and Indigenous America. I clicked on each link to learn more. I was fascinated, knowing about my genetic family tree. I listed so many places, from Europe to the Americas, even Africa, that I was a bit overwhelmed. I was a giant blend of so many, many families! How exciting to know about where I came from!

Chapter 6

The LORD REMEMBERED

And the Lord Remembered

There is this strange phrase in scripture that comes up repeatedly: "the Lord remembered."

The phrase shows up over forty times in the Old Testament, over one hundred times in the Book of Mormon, over thirty times in the New Testament, and over forty times in the Doctrine and Covenants. Of the most curious times the phrase "remembered" is used when it is the Lord that does the remembering. The Lord cannot forget, can He? Perhaps this phrase is saying something more profound than recalling a fact.

A few examples can help us spot a pattern, the most critical pattern about the gathering of Israel. I've highlighted the phrases, but read through them and see if you don't spot the theme. (Let me encourage you here: read all of them. Take a few minutes to absorb what the Lord is saying.)

Old Testament

> *And God remembered Noah*, and every living thing . . . and the waters assuaged.
>
> Genesis 8:1

> *And God remembered Rachel*, and God hearkened to her, and opened her womb.
>
> Genesis 30:22

And God heard their groaning, *and God remembered* his covenant with Abraham, with Isaac, and with Jacob.

Exodus 2:24

He hath remembered his covenant for ever, the word which he commanded to a thousand generations.

Psalm 105:8

Book of Mormon

But behold, there shall be many—at that day when I shall proceed to do a marvelous work among them, *that I may remember* my covenants which I have made unto the children of men, that I may set my hand again the second time to recover my people, which are of the house of Israel.

2 Nephi 29:1

Then shall the great and marvelous things which have been hid up from the foundation of the world from you . . . then shall ye know that *the Father hath remembered* the covenant which he made unto your fathers, O house of Israel.

Ether 4:15

New Testament

To perform the mercy promised to our fathers, *and to remember* his holy covenant; the oath which he sware to our father Abraham.

Luke 1:72–73

He is not here, but is risen: *remember* how he spake unto you when he was yet in Galilee.

Luke 24:6, 8

Now I praise you, brethren, *that ye remember me* in all things, and keep the ordinances, as I delivered them to you.

1 Corinthians 11:2

Doctrine and Covenants

> Search diligently, pray always, and be believing, and all things shall work together for your good, if ye walk uprightly *and remember* the covenant wherewith ye have covenanted one with another.
>
> Doctrine and Covenants 90:24

How uplifting and encouraging is the idea! The Lord remembers us. We see a key that when He covenants with us, He will remember us. He will remember His promises. Over and over again in scripture, we see that the Lord remembered the promises He made in the Abrahamic covenant: posterity, priesthood, prosperity, and a promised land. When Israel was troubled and struggling, the Lord remembered.

The Lord cannot "cognitively" forget something. The "Lord remembered" phrase is more meaningful than just recalling someone. The term means that the Lord recalls His promises in a covenant. As we've discussed all of the scatterings, the exile, and losses, it is profound that the Lord remembers us. He will not forget His covenants.

And that is encouraging.

It is encouraging that despite everything we might do, from the silliest mistake to outright terrible decisions, He will remember us. And part of the remembrance is to bring us home. He will gather us in. Thus, a key to the gathering of Israel is Faith in Jesus Christ. We must believe in Him. We have to have faith that we are worth saving. We must have faith that He loves us, despite anything we do. We must have faith that He can forgive us. We have to have faith He can save us. "I say unto you, that there shall be no other name given nor any other way nor means whereby salvation can come unto the children of men, only in and through the name of Christ, the Lord Omnipotent" (Mosiah 3:17).

A Rainbow, a Sign of the Covenant

As a kid, I focused on the fun and exciting elements of the scripture story. I focused on the animals two by two, or the rain that "came tumbling down," and even the giant ark. There is, however, a key element, a sign that I have glossed over. Yet, this element of the story may be the most profound, the most touching, and the most insightful part. This component teaches us more about the love of God than maybe any other aspect. That profound and poignant element is the sign of the rainbow.

God promises to save us and reminds us of salvation by making the sign of the rainbow. The rainbow is a highlight of the Noah-ark story. Yet, we often focus on so many other specifics that we forget his fundamental symbol, the sign of the covenant.

A bow was a weapon. It is a devastating weapon that causes destruction and death from above. So how does this symbol of ruin remind us of a loving Father in Heaven?

At the beginning of the Noah story, we are told the reason for the flood and destruction of all creation.

> [5] And God saw that the wickedness of man was great in the earth, and that every imagination of the thoughts of his heart was only evil continually. [6] And it repented the Lord that he had made man on the earth, and it grieved him at his heart.
>
> Genesis 6:5–6

Humanity had become wicked, corrupt, and their hearts were always filled with evil. This pained our Creator. Rather than watch another family, another child, be born and grow up in such sin and corruption, He decided to destroy it. We know how the rest of the story goes. The Lord chooses to save a remnant, Noah, and his family. The Lord commands Noah and his family to build an ark. They fill it with representative animals and birds on earth. The Lord closes the door of the ark, and the flood begins. The rains come down, the water bursts from the ground, too. All of creation is covered in water. Only the family and creatures in the ark survive.

Eventually the Lord remembers Noah and the inhabitants of the ark, and the rains stop. Finally, the ark lands, and the people and animals are saved. Then, a curious event happens.

> And Noah builded an altar unto the Lord . . . and offered burnt offerings on the altar. . . . And the Lord said in his heart, I will not again curse the ground any more for man's

> sake; for the imagination of man's heart is evil from his youth; neither will I again smite any more every thing living, as I have done.
>
> Genesis 8:20–21

Before the flood, the Lord saw the evil "in his heart continually." After the flood, the Lord saw the same evil, "the imagination of man's heart is evil from his youth." What changed? Humanity had not changed, and man's heart failed him before the flood. After the flood, the scripture says almost the exact same wording. So, humanity had not changed. What changed? Look again:

"*Noah builded an altar unto the Lord . . . and offered burnt offerings on the altar.*" Humanity didn't change. Because of a covenant, a covenant marked by an altar and sacrifice, a symbol of the atoning sacrifice of Jesus Christ, humanity is saved.

The Lord made a covenant with Noah. The Lord promised not to destroy the world by flood. Not ever again. But what did Noah covenant to do? This is one of those cases where there doesn't seem to be anything required of humanity in this covenant. Noah doesn't have to obey or have faith or participate in any ordinances. This lack of covenant requirement prompts the question, "Why not?" Maybe that's the point.

The Lord is telling us that He will save us. Through the grace of Jesus Christ, we are saved. At the beginning of the scriptural story, the Lord tells us that He promises to save us. We do not save ourselves, work it out on our own, or earn salvation. Rather, our Father has provided a Savior, whose grace is sufficient. We covenant with him, which means He will protect us even when we blow it. His grace will cover our sins. And just in case we forget and think that there is no hope, the Lord puts a sign in the heavens to remind us. In the sky, we see his bow, the reminder that He loves us despite everything we do to the contrary. Using the sign of destruction and power, the Lord reverses its meaning. The bow is no longer a symbol of destruction but love and protection. When we see the sign of the covenant, the rainbow, we remember He will never give up on us.

I Am with Thee

God promises Abraham many significant blessings. One of them is that He will be with Him. I love how this part of the covenant promise is shared with Jacob, Abraham's grandson,

> And, behold, I am with thee, and will keep thee in all places whither thou goest, and will bring thee again into this land; for I will not leave thee, until I have done that which I have spoken to thee of.
>
> Genesis 28:15

Ah, the sublime beauty of this promise. The Lord will be with Jacob and, by extension, all of us, wherever we go. His covenant promises so much, but one part that warms my heart and humbles me is His promise to be with us. "I will not leave thee."

After being sold as a slave by his brothers, Joseph of Egypt is imprisoned. Joseph is falsely accused after working hard to rise in Potiphar's house. In the pit, in his lowest time, we may ask, "Where is the Lord during all of this?" The scripture answers, "But the *Lord was with Joseph,* and shewed him mercy" (Genesis 39:21, emphasis added). The promise the Lord gave to Jacob, he shows with Joseph.

Ezekiel's story is similarly striking. As a priest in training, he worked his whole life to be ordained. Yet, on his birthday—the very day he would be ordained to higher priestly duties—he is found sitting by a canal in Babylon, captured and in exile, far from the temple. Yet, in that moment of separation from the temple, his priestly calling, he receives a vision of God (Ezekiel 1). In the vision, Ezekiel sees the great throne of God. Shockingly, the throne is not in Jerusalem, housed in the temple but on wheels, in the sky above Ezekiel. The merciful Lord shows Ezekiel that He is not contained to the temple in Jerusalem but right there with Ezekiel. During the darkest moments of Ezekiel's exile, the Lord is with him.

Joseph Smith was cast into Liberty Jail, falsely accused, separated from his family and the company of the Saints. Kept in terrible physical conditions. Joseph wrote, "We are kept under strong guard, night and day, . . . food is scant, uniform, and coarse; . . . we have been compelled to sleep on the floor with straw, and not blankets sufficient to keep us warm ."*

In this terrible suffering, Joseph wrote, "O God, where art thou?" The Lord answered, "My son, peace be unto thy soul" (D&C 121:1, 7). Joseph was not alone, but the Lord was there with him. Some of our most powerful scriptures were revealed in Liberty Jail (see sections 121, 122, 123).†

The Psalms echo this desire, this reaching we have to be near the Lord. (I will quote a more modernized translation that highlights this emotion). The Lord promises to each of us He will be near.

> 15 The eyes of the Lord are on the righteous,
> and his ears are open to their cry.
> 17 When the righteous cry for help, the Lord hears,
> and rescues them from all their troubles.
> 18 The Lord is near to the brokenhearted,
> and saves the crushed in spirit.
>
> Psalm 34:15, 17–18, NRSV

In one of the most loving expressions of the blessing of the covenant, we learn that He is with us. The promise of the Abrahamic covenant, the new and everlasting covenant, is that the Lord will always be there for us. He may not remove all of our burdens. He has gifted us with agency and the opportunity to learn. Yet despite everything that may happen and in our lowest moments, He is always near. He is not distant or far away. He has not forgotten us.

Key Ideas to Remember

- "The Lord remembered" is a scriptural phrase that refers to the Lord's covenant promises.

---

* Joseph Smith, "Letter to Isaac Galland, 22 March 1839," in Times and Seasons, Feb. 1840, 52, josephsmithpapers.org. https://abn.churchofjesuschrist.org/study/history/topics/liberty-jail?lang=eng&adobe_mc_ref=https%3A%2F%2Fwww.churchofjesuschrist.org%2Fstudy%2Fhistory%2Ftopics%2Fliberty-jail%3Flang%3Deng&adobe_mc_sdid=SDID%3D7362FA8D2EC86C5C-0B8044A235D4065D%7CMCORGID%

† Jeffrey R. Holland, "Lessons from Liberty Jail," Church Educational System fireside for young adults, Sept. 7, 2008, speeches.byu.edu.

- There is never anything we can do that is so terrible that the Lord will permanently turn from us.
- The rainbow is a token of the Lord's covenant sign that He will always love us. By binding ourselves to the Savior, as symbolized in sacrifice, we will be redeemed.
- A blessing of the covenant is that He will be near us during our darkest times.

Chapter 7

CHOSEN

When Lisa and I were young and just starting kindergarten, we had to draw a story about our lives. It was Back to School Night. Our teacher told us our parents were coming! We diligently worked to ready the classroom, decorating and hanging a welcome sign. We organized our classwork and the classroom to show off everything we had done in our class. We also drew pictures that were going to be the highlight of the evening. Carefully taped to the walls, our works of art would tell our story. Our parents, grandparents, family, or guardians could come and learn about our school. They would also witness our drawings. We would present our pictures in crayon and butcher paper, highlighting the most important things about us.

I have no memory of this event. I was, after all, only four or five years old. However, my mom tells the story of our drawings. She and my dad went to Back to School Night and learned about our class. They saw the books we were reading, the toys we played with, and the little rugs we slept on during nap time. Finally, as the highlight, our drawings were unveiled. (Okay, I may be over telling this, it was only a kindergarten event, but it was a big deal.)

Taped to the wall was my picture. I had created quite the scene about my family. I had drawn row after row of little beds. Row after row of little beds with babies graced my drawing. I had titled my picture "special." I had drawn my childhood understanding of the adoption agency! In my childhood imagination, the agency was a room with row after row of cribs with many babies. Parents could then carefully "shop" and choose their child. I was drawing how I imagined my parents specially chose me.

My mom was mortified. The adoption agency told her not to highlight adoption as special or that we were chosen. Instead, we just came to our parents a different way. She had to sit both of us down and explain a few things. (It might seem odd that my mom talked to both of us when it was my drawing, but one thing we learned about twins is "if one did it, you could be sure the other was going to, too.") First, there was no shopping room full of tiny beds, with babies to be chosen like produce at a supermarket. Second, we were beloved, but being adopted did not make us exceptional. It was just a different way to get to our family. A family was just the beginning—we would have to make something of the opportunity we were given.

Everyone wants to be special. We want to be loved and seen for who we are inside or could be. We hope someone will look past our flaws, glimpse into our hearts, and love and admire who we are deep inside. We long to be seen, known, and loved.

More than anyone, the Lord is the one who loves and sees us. We want to feel that the Lord is aware of us and that He loves us. Like a baby waiting for adoption, we want to be selected, picked, and chosen. Israel was the "chosen people" of the Old Testament. The Nephites are chosen to be led out of Jerusalem before being destroyed. There are many stories of a favorite son being chosen by their parent, from Isaac favoring Esau and Rebekah favoring Jacob (Genesis 25:28) to Jacob favoring Joseph over his other eleven sons (see Genesis 37:3–4). Is this favoritism "being chosen?" Does being "chosen" mean you have a unique advantage in the world? What exactly does it mean to be chosen?

Being Chosen

Scriptures talk a lot about being chosen. We hear Abraham was "chosen" before he was born (see Abraham 3:23). We hear about the house of Israel being the "chosen people." Isaiah 43:21 says, "This people have I formed for myself; they shall shew forth my praise." Later, requoting the same verses, the Apostle Peter says, "Ye are a chosen generation, a royal priesthood, an holy nation, a peculiar people; that ye should shew forth the praises of him who hath called you out of darkness into his marvellous light" (1 Peter 2:9).

I think the best understanding of being "chosen" comes from Deuteronomy. At a critical moment, the Lord speaks to the people. The Israelites are about to become a nation. For the first time, the people of the Lord will become more than just a family, more than enslaved people in Egypt. The Lord speaks to the Israelites, right on the cusp of entering the promised land. They have left Egypt and Pharaoh, they have witnessed the plagues of Egypt, the crossing of the Sea, the Lord on Sinai, and now, after wandering for forty years, they are going to cross into the promised land. At this crucial moment, He says,

> 6 For thou art an holy people unto the Lord thy God: the Lord thy God hath chosen thee to be a special people unto himself, above all people that are upon the face of the earth.
>
> 7 The Lord did not set his love upon you, nor choose you, because ye were more in number than any people; for ye were the fewest of all people:
>
> 8 But because the Lord loved you, and because he would keep the oath which he had sworn unto your fathers, hath the Lord brought you out with a mighty hand, and redeemed you out of the house of bondmen, from the hand of Pharaoh king of Egypt.
>
> 9 Know therefore that the Lord thy God, he is God, the faithful God, which keepeth covenant and mercy with them that love him and keep his commandments to a thousand generations.
>
> Deuteronomy 7:6–9

The Lord tells them they were chosen, not because of anything they did. They were not chosen because they were great or powerful. They were chosen because they "were the fewest of all people." The Lord chose *them not because they were great* but because they were *few.*

Why would the Lord choose a people to serve Him when they were small? Because it is only with the help and blessing of the Lord that they would succeed. Perhaps the Lord wanted there to be no doubt about how Israel prevailed. It was not because of their power but through His. When the Lord chooses the most ordinary people, the small and simple things, it becomes a testimony to the world that He is with them. Only with His power, His blessing, His Spirit, will they become something great.

Small and Simple Things

Helaman teaches his sons the same idea saying,

> Behold I say unto you, that by small and simple things are great things brought to pass; and small means in many instances doth confound the wise. And the Lord God doth work by means to bring about his great and eternal purposes; and by very small means the Lord doth confound the wise and bringeth about the salvation of many souls.
>
> Alma 37:6–7

Being chosen is letting the Lord work within us. He chooses us so that we can do His work. Only through and with Him do we become something chosen.

Perhaps the best way to understand the idea of being chosen is to answer, "What are we chosen for?" The calling of Abraham gives us an answer. When Abraham is called of God, the Lord promises many blessings. God tells Abraham He will make him a great nation to serve the nations (Genesis 12:3, 22:18, Galatians 3:7–9, Revelation 7:9–11, D&C 86:11). Amazing! Abraham is blessed, and he receives blessings to turn around and bless everyone else.

Tender Mercies Promised to the Chosen

There is another group, one carved out from the larger, a remnant, that the Lord chose, the family of Lehi. As Nephi begins his record, he ends the first chapter with a significant them:

> But behold, I Nephi, will show unto you that the tender mercies of the Lord are over all those whom he hath chosen,

because of their faith, to make them mighty even unto the power of deliverance."

1 Nephi 1:20

This is the very first chapter of 1 Nephi! I always feel like this is Nephi's mission statement, his thesis, for the entire record. Nephi wants to show us two key ideas:

1. The Lord blesses His chosen with tender mercies.
2. The Lord chose the Nephites because of their faith, which saved them.

Nephi is teaching us about his experiences with the Lord. He and his family were chosen because of their faith. They acted when the Lord asked them to leave. They believed, made great personal sacrifices, and were delivered from destruction. The key was their faith in the Lord Jesus Christ.

It wasn't just deliverance that Nephi learned was a blessing of being chosen. He learned about all the many blessings He was willing to give them. He called them "tender mercies." It was not just one big act that the Lord gifted them. It was daily blessings, too. They were given guidance with the Liahona. They were shown visions and insights into the purpose of life. They were blessed temporally with food and protection. They were instructed to build bows, ships, and new civilizations. The Lord's tender mercies extended to every part of their lives, from simple to great. Being chosen is a promise of God helping and guiding every aspect of our life.

Chosen and the Priesthood

34 Behold, there are many called, but few are chosen. And why are they not chosen?

35 Because their hearts are set so much upon the things of this world, and aspire to the honors of men, that they do not learn this one lesson—

36 That the rights of the priesthood are inseparably connected with the powers of heaven, and that the powers of heaven

cannot be controlled nor handled only upon the principles of righteousness.

37 That they may be conferred upon us, it is true; but when we undertake to cover our sins, or to gratify our pride, our vain ambition, or to exercise control or dominion or compulsion upon the souls of the children of men, in any degree of unrighteousness, behold, the heavens withdraw themselves; the Spirit of the Lord is grieved; and when it is withdrawn, Amen to the priesthood or the authority of that man.

Doctrine and Covenants 121:34–37

Joseph Smith received this revelation while in Liberty Jail. Joseph learned about being chosen while being in jail. Imprisoned and suffering, he discovered that being chosen is about loving others. It is about lifting the downtrodden, helping those that are hurting. It is as if the priesthood is given so that we can act in an extension of the Lord. His hands become our hands. We lift the weak. We carry those who struggle. We give comfort, aid, and love. We minister.

As members of The Church of Jesus Christ of Latter-day Saints, we all have responsibilities and blessings administered by the authority of the priesthood. The priesthood isn't just giving blessings. It is acting in the name of our Lord. "The blessings of the priesthood are available to every righteous man and woman."* We can receive the blessings of the priesthood, but we also have the responsibilities. And that means serving as He would serve.

Being chosen then is not elitist. Instead, it is the way the Lord starts His work of salvation: one at a time so that we, in turn, can help others. John Bytheway says, "First, being 'chosen' doesn't mean we're chosen to sit on thrones and be admired. It's more like being chosen to mow the lawn or bring in the harvest. We're chosen to work, chosen

* Sheri L. Dew, as quoted in *Daughters in My Kingdom: The History and Work of Relief Society* (2017), 127.

to accomplish a difficult mission, chosen to 'bear the ministry' to all the world." †

Being chosen is acting and serving as He would. And that makes sense. The Chosen One is the Savior. He is the prophet, priest, and King promised to all of Israel. While on the cross, He was mocked: "And the people stood beholding. And the rulers also with them derided him, saying, He saved others; let him save himself, if he be Christ, the chosen of God" (Luke 23:35). It was said in ridicule, but He is the Chosen One. His life was an example to us of how to live. His atoning sacrifice saved us from sin and death. We learn to follow Him and walk the disciple's path by being chosen and emulating Him.

KEY IDEAS TO REMEMBER

- The Lord has chosen us.
- It is often the "small and simple" things the Lord uses to work His wonders.
- There is never anything we can do that is so terrible that the Lord will turn from us.
- The priesthood is serving as He would.
- Being chosen means we are "chosen to serve."

† John Bytheway, "Don't Just "Get Through 2 Nephi: Get Something From It!," *Latter-Day Saint Magazine*, February 19, 2008.

Chapter 8

WHO AM I? PATRIARCHAL BLESSING

Receiving My Patriarchal Blessing

When I was fifteen, I received my patriarchal blessing. I had heard a Young Women's lesson about it, teaching me that it would tell me about special promises. The Lord would speak to me and tell me my lineage. This was exciting. I knew the family I grew up with, and they were great. What else would I learn about my roots, where I came from, and my destiny?

Growing up adopted was great, don't get me wrong. I love my family (I'll probably say that a few more times, and I mean it). But there was always a sense of mystery about my genealogical roots. What would I find? In my more ridiculous moments, I imagined I was somebody special, like royalty, hidden away. Maybe one day, I would learn my heritage and take my proper place one day. Like a hero of old, one day, I would discover that I was the hidden heir (gasp!), and my royal nature would be revealed.

Of course, in my more practical moments, I realized that I was probably just an average person with a rich heritage, but most likely average in most regards. While my adoption was closed—meaning the birth and adopted parents do not know each other and information is restricted between them—we knew a little information.

We knew that my birth mom had been a young teenager, fifteen or sixteen years old. The couple was in high school and made a wise decision to give us up. Being the parents of twins couldn't be easy, even as an adult. Being teenagers raising twins would have been a colossal task. I never begrudged them the decision. It seemed like a sacrifice to give up a child to another family, and I never felt abandoned.

You probably have adoption in your family. Everyone feels differently and has a different experience. My twin probably has a different experience from me, so if your experience as a birth parent, adopted parent, adopted family, or adoptee is different—that's okay. Like the rest of our lives, every experience is different for each of us. For me, being adopted meant I was wanted. My parents and grandparents had had many experiences, leading them to us. But I'll save that story for later.

For now, I was headed off to receive my patriarchal blessing. This was it! I was about to find out critical pieces of information about my identity. I would learn things only the Lord knew about me, nature, and eternal destiny. I was going to find out more about who I was.

Who We Are

Understanding who we are is critical. We have many methods of identity today. We are linked to our associations, like our family, city, and nation we are born in, and our ethnic identities. We are described who we are by our career and job. We say, "I'm an engineer" or "I'm a teacher." We also have an eternal identity.

The Lord also has ways of identifying us. These identities can tell us about ourselves and the missions of which we are a part. While the Lord does not have a "set in stone" destiny mapped out, we have agency. He does know more about us and our character and responsibilities than anyone else. Receiving a patriarchal blessing is how the Lord tells us about His plans for us.

The key element of a Patriarchal Blessing is the declaration of our lineage. And that is critical to the gathering of Israel. The gathering of Israel is such a vital component of the plan of salvation that anything that explains our role is indispensable. The critical application of declaring our lineage is to 1) tell us of the blessings for which we may qualify and 2) tell us our responsibilities. It's that last part we sometimes forget. It is easy to focus on all the blessings and forget that we have requirements, obligations, and duties.

There are a few key places where the Lord's people are given their identity. The first is in Genesis 39, when Jacob blesses his sons. Moses gives a similar patriarchal blessing to the tribes before crossing into the promised land in Deuteronomy 33. Lehi gives his sons blessings, highlighting some of their strengths and challenges in 2 Nephi 1–4. Receiving and studying our patriarchal blessings will tell us the Lord's blessings and responsibilities for us. There are unique responsibilities for the tribes, and some are specific to the gathering.

> 1 And Jacob called unto his sons, and said, *Gather* yourselves together, that I may tell you that which shall befall you in the last days.
>
> 2 *Gather* yourselves together, and hear, ye sons of Jacob; and hearken unto Israel your father.
>
> 3 Reuben, thou art my firstborn, my might, and the beginning of my strength, the excellency of dignity, and the excellency of power:
>
> 4 Unstable as water, thou shalt not excel; because thou wentest up to thy father's bed; then defiledst thou it: he went up to my couch.
>
> 5 Simeon and Levi are brethren; instruments of cruelty are in their habitations.
>
> 6 O my soul, come not thou into their secret; unto their assembly, mine honour, be not thou united: for in their anger they slew a man, and in their self will they digged down a wall.
>
> 7 Cursed be their anger, for it was fierce; and their wrath, for it was cruel: I will divide them in Jacob, and scatter them in Israel.
>
> 8 Judah, thou art he whom thy brethren shall praise: thy hand shall be in the neck of thine enemies; thy father's children shall bow down before thee.

9 Judah is a lion's whelp: from the prey, my son, thou art
gone up: he stooped down, he couched as a lion, and as an
old lion; who shall rouse him up?

10 The sceptre shall not depart from Judah, nor a lawgiver
from between his feet, until Shiloh come; and unto him shall
the *gathering* of the people be.

11 Binding his foal unto the vine, and his ass's colt unto the
choice vine; he washed his garments in wine, and his clothes
in the blood of grapes:

12 His eyes shall be red with wine, and his teeth white with
milk.

13 Zebulun shall dwell at the haven of the sea; and he shall
be for an haven of ships; and his border shall be unto Zidon.

14 Issachar is a strong ass couching down between two
burdens:

15 And he saw that rest was good, and the land that it was
pleasant; and bowed his shoulder to bear, and became a
servant unto tribute.

16 Dan shall judge his people, as one of the tribes of Israel.

17 Dan shall be a serpent by the way, an adder in the
path, that biteth the horse heels, so that his rider shall fall
backward.

18 I have waited for thy salvation, O Lord.

19 Gad, a troop shall overcome him: but he shall overcome at
the last.

20 Out of Asher his bread shall be fat, and he shall yield royal
dainties.

21 Naphtali is a hind let loose: he giveth goodly words.

22 Joseph is a fruitful bough, even a fruitful bough by a well;
whose branches run over the wall:

> [23] The archers have sorely grieved him, and shot at him, and hated him:
>
> [24] But his bow abode in strength, and the arms of his hands were made strong by the hands of the mighty God of Jacob; (from thence is the shepherd, the stone of Israel:)
>
> [25] Even by the God of thy father, who shall help thee; and by the Almighty, who shall bless thee with blessings of heaven above, blessings of the deep that lieth under, blessings of the breasts, and of the womb:
>
> [26] The blessings of thy father have prevailed above the blessings of my progenitors unto the utmost bound of the everlasting hills: they shall be on the head of Joseph, and on the crown of the head of him that was separate from his brethren.
>
> [27] Benjamin shall ravin as a wolf: in the morning he shall devour the prey, and at night he shall divide the spoil.
>
> [28] All these are the twelve tribes of Israel: and this is it that their father spake unto them, and blessed them; every one according to his blessing he blessed them.
>
> [29] And he charged them, and said unto them, I am to be gathered unto my people.
>
> Genesis 49:1–28, emphases added

Before the patriarch Jacob died, he gathered his family together to bless them. Like his parents before him, he sought out the covenant and wanted to pass that onto them. The rich heritage, the promises of prosperity, posterity, priesthood, and land, were all things Jacob wanted his family to seek after. He knew that each of his sons found mighty tribes.

Would they also seek after the Lord? He could see strengths and weaknesses, blessings, and failings in each of them. In each of them, he could, as prophet and patriarch, see what they could and would become. In Genesis 49, we peer into their futures (our pasts) to see what they would decide.

Ancient Blessings

The chapter lists all the sons of Jacob, and they are the twelve tribes of Israel. A couple of exciting details jump out at us. First, they are listed in birth order. The birth order was important because the oldest son typically received special blessings, the birthright. However, this will not be the case. Let's earmark that idea, and we'll come back to it.

Next, we remember that the tribes of Israel are named after Jacob's sons, including Joseph's two sons. Joseph's sons, Ephraim and Manasseh, are not listed in this list, just Joseph. Omitting the grandsons keeps the list at twelve. Pro tip: you'll notice that it actually makes thirteen sons and grandsons. One of Leah's children, Levi, becomes a special dedication to the Lord. Numbers 1:39 reminds us of this when Moses is marching around with the Israelites after they have been rescued from bondage in Egypt.

> But the Levites after the tribe of their fathers were not numbered among them. For the LORD had spoken unto Moses, saying, Only thou shalt not number the tribe of Levi, neither take the sum of them among the children of Israel: But thou shalt appoint the Levites over the tabernacle of testimony.
>
> Numbers 1: 47–50

You might notice other lists of the twelve tribes list Ephraim and Manasseh, and Levi. Moses' blessing in Deuteronomy 33 is a perfect example. Sometimes, scripture lists leave Levi out of the list to make it twelve. Other times they'll say "Joseph," not listing the two grandsons. However, when it is listed, it refers to the twelve.

Many members of The Church of Jesus Christ of Latter-day Saints have received their patriarchal blessings. They are frequently from the tribes of Joseph, either Ephraim or Manasseh. When we look at the blessings in scripture, the lists, it can be tricky. Which name are we looking for? However, Joseph, Ephraim, or Manasseh is listed—it is the same thing. In your study, if you see Joseph, you can look at those blessings and responsibilities if you are of the tribe of Ephraim or Manasseh.

What Is in the Blessing?

Jacob is blessing his children. This is more than just a prayer. It is a blessing that brings them into the covenant. It also tells them about their futures, rights, and, most importantly, their responsibilities. If Jacob is blessing his children with the promises of the covenant and telling them about their own lives, we should look at what it has to say.

Jacob blesses all of his sons. However, the gathering of Israel has specific references to the tribes of Judah and Joseph. The sections on Judah and Joseph are also the longest, by far. This isn't to say that the other tribes are lesser. The tribes of Israel are significant to the Lord. If your patriarchal blessing indicates you have the blessings from one of the others, that is a rare gift. It is precious, and we should embrace that and study it, too. I merely point out that here, in Genesis 49, while we are blessed, there are a few extra points we should look at about those two groupings. Instead, let's follow the clues that Judah and Joseph are underscored for a reason, and we'll want to dive into their specific blessings to see what they are about and why.

Let's do a deep dive.

Shema

After gathering his family, Jacob invokes the word "hearken." It is easy to read right past the opening phrases to get to the heart of the excerpt. In this case, the first word is exceptionally relevant. Hearken is not a word we use today, so its meaning may not be immediately apparent. Hearken means listen, like a command. Think of it like, "Listen!" or "Hey, pay attention!" It also has the idea of action. Embedded in the word is the concept of "get ready" and "obey." When I hear the word "hearken," it tells me to pay close attention and get ready to do something. I mentally replace the word hearken with "listen and do something about it."

The term in Hebrew is *Shema* and will later become a prayer (Numbers 6:4–9, 11:13–21, Numbers 15:37–41).* The Shema is a prayer that is said multiple times daily, reminding our Jewish brothers

---

* Brown, S. Driver, and C. Briggs, *The Brown-Driver-Briggs Hebrew and English Lexicon* (Boston: Hendrickson Publishers, 2004), entry 8088.

and sisters of the unity of God and the importance of remembering Him.

Hearken isn't just a term that is used in the Old Testament. The Lord uses hearken in many scriptures. Hearken becomes a standard introduction and theme in Doctrine and Covenants, with the prologue and epilogue starting with the word "hearken" (D&C 1:1, D&C 133:1). There is the word hearken in the first verse of the scripture of this dispensation. The Lord starts His prologue to the Doctrine and Covenants with the idea that we should listen and get ready to act. It seems especially notable that in our day, the Lord starts his revelations to us with this word, "Hearken!" In this blessing in Genesis 49, Jacob tells his family (and all of us) to pay attention. We are going to learn something important and must act.

At this point, we want to jump into these blessings and see what is in store for the children of Israel. But we are not quite ready yet. We need to lay a little more foundation to see its relevance and importance when we do study the blessing.

Ancient Scripture: Repetition

Ancient scripture is dense. Its style is not exactly like our writing style. In modern writing, we tend to take our time, explain things in detail, and give lots of clues to a building conclusion. It is easy to pick up on themes and ideas in modern styles because we have grown up learning how to recognize them. A current talk or essay has a thesis and usually has phrases like, "now I'm going to tell you about three things," and then uses those three supporting ideas to support the thesis. We have all heard the old, "tell them what you're going to tell them, tell them, then tell them that you told them." We repeat, we show over and over, and we explain carefully. Modern writing also has chapters, paragraphs, and sentences, helping us understand when ideas are new or building on one another. Ancient scripture moves faster and uses different techniques or "clues" to highlight the point.

One method is using repeated words or phrases. Those repeated words or phrases are like "hyperlinks" that connect other ideas. Much like our "zoomed in" and "zoomed out" approach of Genesis, repeated words tie different stories together, helping us link ideas and create themes. Scripture relies on us to pick up on repeated phrases and hyperlinks, and we have to watch for repeated words. Like the other tools of structure and meaning of names, repeated words teach us the critical concepts being taught.

My Hour Is Not Yet Come

Let's look at an example the Savior used. In the gospel of John, the Savior repeats a phrase, "my hour is not yet come." When His mother asks Him to help at the wedding and Cana, He reminds her, "Mine hour has not yet come" (John 2:4). That's the first time we hear it, and it is a little curious. What does the Lord mean? It is not immediately apparent. Is He saying He cannot help his mother at the wedding at Cana? The Savior does help His mother. He does bring blessing and abundance to a wedding—a symbol of His covenant relationship with us. However, He performs a miracle, yet the meaning of His comment, "mine hour is not yet come," seems to conflict. He performs a miracle, but His time hasn't come? We must turn to examine the use of repetition to understand His meaning.

The Lord uses this exact phrase the next time he speaks to his stepbrothers. They have come to encourage the Lord to go to Judea rather than stay in the small towns of Galilee. He reminds them, "My time is not yet here; for you any time will do. . . . My time has not yet fully come" (John 7:6, 8, NIV). In that same chapter, the phrase is repeated one more time as we learn, "No one laid hands on him, because his hour had not yet come" (John 7:30, NIV).

Now we're building on an idea. The Lord's ministry began with teaching, preaching, and performing wonders. Yet "His time" is not part of that but something else for which we are waiting. We ask ourselves, "What time is He talking about?" The repeating phrase continues, enticing us to keep searching and keep asking. When people seek to capture Him, we learn next, "Yet no one seized Him because His hour had not yet come" (John 8:20, NIV). When several non-Jews, Greeks, seek to learn from Him, the Lord tells Philip, "The hour has come" (John 12:23, NIV). Interestingly, now at this stage of His ministry, the "hour" is here. Why, what is different? The end of the chapter gives us the clue we need. "Now my soul is troubled, and what shall I say? 'Father, save me from this hour? . . . Now is the time" (John 12:27, 31, NIV). We learn what He means about "His time." He says, "Jesus knew that the hour had come for Him to leave this world" (John 13:1, NIV).

The beginning of the Atonement of Jesus Christ is "His time." The moment all creation had waited for had finally arrived. The climax of this repeating phrase comes in the Lord's High Priestly Intercessory Prayer, "Father, the hour has come" (John 17:1, NIV). In a brilliant and careful repetition of words, John concludes that the Atonement of Christ is the "time" for which all creation has been waiting. All points of His mission, His teaching, preaching, miracles, and parable telling pointed to this incredible moment. This repetition of words leads us to the truth: Jesus is the Christ.

FAMILY, COVENANT RESPONSIBILITY, GATHERING

Jacob's patriarchal blessing to his sons, the tribes of Israel, uses repetition on three ideas: family, covenant responsibility, and gathering. The story moves so fast that we would miss it if we didn't slow down, savor it, and notice the clues. Let's look at them together to see how gathering, family, and covenant blessings are all packed into this chapter.

GATHER

We should first notice one of our main themes: gathering. In this short set of verses (Genesis 49:1–28), the word "gather" is used three times. THREE TIMES! Did you see it? Go back and see if you can spot the three times. (I'll wait.) I highlighted them, so it is easy to spot in that fairly lengthy pericope (see pages 101–103).

He starts by saying, "Gather yourselves together, that I may tell you that which shall befall you in the last days" (Genesis 49:1) and "Gather yourselves together, and hear, ye sons of Jacob; and hearken unto Israel your father" (Genesis 49:2). He begins the section on blessings by first telling them he is gathering. Who is He gathering? He starts by gathering his children and grandchildren around him. He even begins by saying, "Israel your father," giving us a framework for the blessing.

Inclusio

When scripture uses a phrase at the beginning and the end of various verses, it is called an inclusio. The inclusio is a "nerd word" or a technical term. An inclusio serves as "bookends" to highlight the theme of that section. It can be a phrase or an entire verse that repeats, and that bracketing gives us an important literary structure to highlight a theme. In this case, the underlying point of Genesis 49 and Jacob's blessings is the gathering of God's family.

This gathering is going to be on multiple levels. First, this is a father giving blessings and direction to his children. He reminds them of the relational nature of this blessing by also repeating this three times (see verses 1, 2, and 28, also serving as an *inclusio).* Second, it is also a pattern for our Heavenly Father to bless us, His children. He reviewed how and what Jacob says to his sons will tell us something that the Lord may want to tell us.

The repetition and use of an *inclusio* reinforce the idea of a gathering. Jacob is gathering his own family. He is concerned for their welfare. He wants to protect, bless, and teach them in the ways of the Lord. Just as Jacob gathers his own family, the Lord wants to gather His family. All of humanity is God's children, and He loves and cares for each of us. He wants to gather each child, family, and tribe into His embrace. He wants to protect, bless, and teach them His ways, so they can flourish and be happy.

Family

We talk about family often in gospel settings. We speak of the importance of family, sing "Families are Forever," and have "The Family: A Proclamation." The beginning of our earthy existence starts with the creation of a family, Adam and Eve. The blessings of the covenant are given to one family, Abraham and Sarah. Family is how the Lord works with us! The new and everlasting covenant brings us into God's family, returning us to His presence. He works with us one at a time and in families.

When the Lord binds Himself to humanity, He does it with a family. First Adam, but we see it with Noah, too. Then Abraham and on and on. Now, we have Jacob blessing his family. The Lord could have chosen anyone. He could have just . . . picked people. Instead, he works through a family. I think God wants to show us that our greatest happiness is in the family. And His greatest happiness is in His family—us!

Jacob is going to bless his family here. And we are part of that great big family, the sometimes-messed-up-sometimes-brilliant family of Abraham. We are the family of Abraham. There is one other testament to the love God finds in the family. Of all the titles God chooses to go by, the one most common is Father.

Covenant Responsibility

The last repeating idea that is highlighted is the responsibilities that come with these blessings. We have already touched on the idea of being chosen. Being chosen means we receive blessings so that we may serve God and bless others. The patriarchal blessings also give the tribes their specific responsibilities. Let's look at those next.

Key Ideas to Remember

- Patriarchal blessings can declare our lineage as the house of Israel.
- Ancient blessings are still be fulfilled today, in us.
- Hearken is a term that is more than just listening. It is about taking action.
- Scripture uses techniques like repetition and inclusio to teach us eternal principles.
- God includes us in His family.
- We have rights and responsibilities as the modern-day house of Israel.

Chapter 9

WHAT IS *in a* NAME?

I was given the name Dawn when I was born. My twin was Desiree. I don't remember being called Dawn or hearing Lisa called Desiree. As we were in foster care for just a few months, I was too little to remember being called by that name. After being placed in foster care, we were adopted. My parents gave us new names: Lori Lyn and Lisa Lyn Denning. We still knew our birth names but were now Dennings.

Names are fascinating. It is how we are known our whole life, yet we do not choose them. They are selected for us. Some names are given because they are popular in the family. Babies are given the names of their fathers or mothers or perhaps grandparents. Other times babies are given names of other important people or to remember friends. Some names are religious in nature and recall prophets and heroes, men and women of great faith. Other times the names are truly unique like the child is meant to be, making their own name and mark on the world.

At times in our lives, we may be given or called different names. I have been called many variations of Lori Denning throughout my life. To my friends, I am Lori. I have been called Miss or Ms. Denning on various more formal occasions. I have also been Sister Denning at church. On my mission, I was Hermana Denning. I have also been called nicknames like "Wo" when Lisa and I couldn't pronounce the letter "l" or 'r," so Lori became "whoa-whee," but shortened to "Wo." Lisa was equally hard to say, so, as a little kid, I dropped the "Li" and couldn't' say "s," and she became 'Ta.' Wo and Ta were our names for years. Rick and Mike, our older brothers, still call us that from time to time. I love the nickname way more than being called "Ms. Denning." It is all in the association.

Each of the names has a certain meaning, a nuance to it. Like "Wo" reminds me of the love of a family and childhood innocence. If you call me Ms. Denning, it typically means you do not know me. Hermana Denning immediately transports me to when I wore a name tag.

Once I was adopted, I became Lori. It is the name by which I am known. It is the name I think of when I think of myself.

Names and Narratives

The names of the sons of Israel are insightful and unique. They tell us about their blessings, challenges, and their eternal potential. It isn't typical for us to look at the meaning of names today, but anciently it revealed a great deal.

We want to know all about the characters when we read a story. We long to understand their backstory, motivations, and how they got to today. Knowing a person's reasons makes them intriguing. Yet, in ancient scripture, we do not get background very much. Ancient narrative and stories left a lot of that detail out.

One way scripture authors told us about people and their backstory is the meaning of their names. Anciently names revealed vital characteristics and attributes about the person. Knowing a person's name gave you power, knowledge, and even a sense of intimacy.* A change or an addition of a name could indicate a change in circumstances.† A name was not only stated the characteristics the person had, but it could also be aspirational.

A person's name could be key to understanding the person's nature or role in the plan of salvation. For example, Noah means "rest," as we've already discussed. Israel means one who wrestles with God and

---

* Walter A. Elwell, *Evangelical Dictionary of Biblical Theology*, electronic ed., Baker Reference Library (Grand Rapids: Baker Book House, 1996), 406.

† Elwell.

prevails (Geneses 32:28). Enoch means dedicated, which is apt for a prophet dedicating his life and all of Zion to God.‡

Ancient narratives give us clues into the motivations and aspirations of characters by the meaning of their names. Names can also be revelatory, indicating something that will happen in that child's day and future.

For the sons of Israel, their names are critically important. Here are a few key names and their meanings.

- Joseph: Added, he shall be added upon§
- Manasseh: God has made me forget (Genesis 41:51)
- Ephraim: Fruitful, or two fruit land (Genesis 41:52)¶
- Judah: Praise Yhwh or Praise Jehovah

Place names work the same way, often indicating something spiritual or noteworthy has happened there. Here are a few notable examples:

- Jerusalem: Foundation of peace
- Bethel: House of God (Genesis 35:1–5), where Jacob had a vision of a ramp or ladder leading into heaven and the Lord on top of it.
- Peniel: Face of God (Genesis 32:32, Hosea 12:4), where Jacob had a vision of God and wrestled an angel.
- Bethlehem: House of Bread, where Jesus was born, the Bread of Life
- Nauvoo: They are beautiful

The Blessing of Israel

Jacob blesses each son, telling of some of their challenges and their futures. The blessings may give insights into the specific son and disclose that tribe's future. One way this is indicated is Jacob uses highly

‡ Chad Brand et al., eds., "Enoch," *Holman Illustrated Bible Dictionary* (Nashville, TN: Holman Bible Publishers, 2003), 489.

§ Daniel C. Browning Jr., "Joseph," ed. Chad Brand et al., *Holman Illustrated Bible Dictionary* (Nashville, TN: Holman Bible Publishers, 2003), 947.

¶ Browning, 499–500.

metaphorical language. He uses a lot of comparison and imagery. For example, he called Judah a "lion's whelp" (Genesis 49:9) and Joseph a "fruitful bough . . . branches run over the wall" (Genesis 49:22). Judah is not a baby lion, and Joseph is not, in reality, a tree branch. There must be something else we are to understand from these symbols.

Judah

The first tribe that gets the most discussion is Judah. Judah and Joseph get the most verses, the most extended blessings, the most "air time." Lengthy treatment may indicate we need to dig deeper in scripture and discover more is here.

Judah is going to be the ruler of the twelve tribes. Kings David and Solomon come from Judah and are promised to rule forever (2 Sam 7). We see the allusions to rulership with a lion, a mighty beast. The symbol of a scepter also denotes kingship. More scripture highlights this blessing and eventuality (including Psalms 2 and 89; Isaiah 11:1–16; Jeremiah 33:15; Amos 9:1–14; 2 Nephi 21). The Messiah is promised from this line, who is Jesus of Nazareth (Luke 1:32–33; Romans 1:3; Revelation 22:16).

Judah's personal story is also recounted right in this section of Genesis. His failings and challenges he faced earlier in his life, including his plot to kill his younger brother Joseph, are redeemed. In the Joseph story, we see Judah as a changed man. The same person who plotted to kill his younger brother (Genesis 37:26–27) offers himself as a sacrifice for Benjamin. When Judah, now older and changed, meets Joseph-in-disguise, he makes the right decision. He saves his younger brother Benjamin like he should have when Joseph was at risk. Judah becomes a savior to his family. As protector and redeemer of his family, Judah is given the blessing of the ruling (Genesis 37–38).

Ultimately, Jesus Christ has inherited the right to rule over all creation (Hebrews 7:14). As the birthright son of Judah, the son of David who is the King of all (Matthew 1:1).

Joseph

The blessings promised to Joseph are impressive.

> [22] Joseph is a fruitful bough, even a fruitful bough by a well; whose branches run over the wall:
>
> [23] The archers have sorely grieved him, and shot at him, and hated him:
>
> [24] But his bow abode in strength, and the arms of his hands were made strong by the hands of the mighty God of Jacob; (from thence is the shepherd, the stone of Israel:)
>
> [25] Even by the God of thy father, who shall help thee; and by the Almighty, who shall bless thee with blessings of heaven above, blessings of the deep that lieth under, blessings of the breasts, and of the womb:
>
> [26] The blessings of thy father have prevailed above the blessings of my progenitors unto the utmost bound of the everlasting hills: they shall be on the head of Joseph, and on the crown of the head of him that was separate from his brethren.
>
> Genesis 49:22–26

Joseph's first blessings are all about abundance. He is called a fruitful branch, a fruitful branch by a well, growing so much that it cannot be contained and bursts over its enclosing wall. Being "fruitful" is one of the blessings of Eden and the new and everlasting covenant (Moses 2:28; Genesis 1:22, 17:6, 41:52; Leviticus 26:9). His "fruit" can be his family. Ephraim does prosper as a tribe with some of the most extensive lands and family members.

Joseph's family and blessing will be like a branch that grows and extends over a wall. Can you think of any examples of the family of Joseph "branching out" and scattering throughout the world? Lehi's family! Lehi's family is from Manasseh and marries Ishmael's family from Ephraim. The Lehites are the line of Joseph. Additionally, the Book of Mormon, a record of the house of Joseph, is carried to all the world. The history of the covenants and promises of the Lord are not just in the Bible but in Joseph's family record, too.

There are many notable Josephs: Joseph of Egypt, Joseph son of Lehi, Joseph Smith Sr., and Joseph Smith Jr. The role of Joseph Smith Jr. in the gathering of Israel is undeniable. He was "fruitful" and ushered in the Restoration. His "adding" or restoration of the covenants of the Lord, the Book of Mormon, Doctrine and Covenants, and Pearl of Great Price enhanced the ancient canon. Joseph Smith said, "I was called of my Heavenly Father to lay a foundation in this great work and kingdom in this dispensation and testify His revealed will to scattered Israel."*

Ephraim

Jacob's blessing also highlights Ephraim. Ephraim receives the birthright in Genesis 48 (see also 1 Chronicles 5:1–2; Jeremiah 31:9). In the previous chapter, Ephraim, the younger son, receives birthright instead of Manasseh. The common theme is that the younger son gets the birthright instead of the older one. From Cain and Abel, Nephi instead of Laman, David instead of all his brothers, and Jacob instead of Esau, Ephraim is just another in a long line of examples of younger sons receiving the birthright.

The younger son inheriting reminds us that the Lord gives blessings. The rules established by convention and culture, as in the rule of the birthright, are not maintained by the Lord. He blesses those with whom He covenants. The Lord directs and blesses humanity so that all may flourish. He receives a double portion of land as an inheritance (Genesis 48:21–22). This double portion, the extra blessing of the land, is given to bless the rest of the family.

---

* Joseph Smith Jr., "Discourse to Saints, July 1843"; History of the Church (commonly called Documentary History of the Church) 5:516.

Our Responsibilities

We receive blessings so that we may lift and bless others. One of the great blessings of this dispensation of the house of Israel is the priesthood.

> Therefore, thus saith the Lord unto you, with whom the priesthood hath continued through the lineage of your fathers—for ye are lawful heirs, according to the flesh, and have been from the world with Christ in God.
>
> D&C 86: 8–9

Ephraim is given blessings and responsibilities. Joseph Fielding Smith explained our rights and responsibilities this way.

> The members of the Church, most of us of the tribe of Ephraim, are of the remnant of Jacob. We know it to be the fact that the Lord called upon the descendants of Ephraim to commence his work in the earth in these last days. We know further that he has said that he set Ephraim, according to the promises of his birthright, at the head. Ephraim receives the "richer blessings," these blessings being those of presidency or direction. The keys are with Ephraim. It is Ephraim who is to be endowed with power to bless and give to the other tribes, including the Lamanites, their blessings. All the other tribes of Jacob, including the Lamanites, are to be crowned with glory in Zion by the hands of Ephraim. . . .
>
> That the remnants of Joseph, found among the descendants of Lehi, will have part in this great work is certainly consistent, and the great work of this restoration, the building of the temple and the City of Zion, or New Jerusalem, will fall to the lot of the descendants of Joseph, but it is Ephraim who will stand at the head and direct the work.†

† Joseph Fielding Smith, *Doctrines of Salvation,* 2:250–51; italics in original removed.

Blessings of the Messiah

It is also our blessing and responsibility to gather Israel and all the nations. We gather them to the Lord, to the truth, and to share the blessings of exaltation.

> That all the ends of the earth may know that we, thy servants, have heard thy voice, and that thou hast sent us; that from among all these, thy servants, the sons of Jacob, may gather out the righteous. . . . And may all the scattered remnants of Israel, who have been driven to the ends of the earth, come to a knowledge of the truth, believe in the Messiah, and be redeemed from oppression, and rejoice before thee.
>
> D&C 109:57–58, 67

Once again, we see that we receive blessings to help others. The blessings promised are beautiful, powerful, and inspiring. The good news of the gospel of Jesus Christ is our message, and freedom and joy are our promises. In order to have joy, we are instructed in both the blessings we are offered and the responsibility we have to share them:

- Gather scattered remnants of Israel
- Teach the truth of the Lord
- Preach faith in the Messiah
- Invite all into redemption from oppression

When we receive the declaration of our lineage in a patriarchal blessing, we have insights into who we are and who we could become. We may learn more about our lineage and to what we are heirs. It is exactly like finding out we are (gasp!) the heir to the kingdom all along. We are the birthright children of Abraham. We are of the house of Jacob. Most likely, we are from the house of Joseph. We are promised all the blessings of Abraham, including the priesthood, so that we may serve and lift others. We are also called to gather scattered Israel and all the world. The message and blessings of the Messiah are ours, and it's our great calling to share with our brothers and sisters.

Key Ideas to Remember

- We are heirs to the kingdom of God.
- We are given many blessings that will help us complete our mission to bring all to Christ. Our rights and responsibilities are indicated in scripture and our patriarchal blessing.
- The tribe of Judah inherits the right of rulership. Christ is our ultimate King, ruling forever.
- The tribes of Joseph, Ephraim, and Manasseh, are called explicitly to gather Israel.
- We are to gather a remnant, bringing them the Messiah's blessing of freedom and redemption.

PART 4: GATHERING

Approved for Adoption

The Children's Home Society had finally approved my parents for adoption. After months of applications, interviews with psychologists, home visits, and more, they got word that they could receive a baby one day. They were delighted and excited. They had told everyone in the ward, their friends, family, neighbors, and work colleagues about their good news. Everyone shared in their joy that someday another baby would join the Denning family. With two older boys, the family would soon be three children.

Or would it? They were told it might take years for a baby to become available. They should hope but not expect to hear anything for months or years. They patiently went back about their lives, hoping for the day when a call would come.

Only a few months later, my mom, Lynda, and grandmother, Ileen, were spending the day shopping. They drove from store to store together, shared their company, and had a great afternoon laughing. While they drove, Ileen admitted something to my mom. "I had a dream last night."

"Oh?" Lynda responded.

"This wasn't a normal dream. This dream was special," My grandmother Ileen said. She had always felt a connection to the spiritual. Her mother felt the same way. They both felt like they had glimpses of eternity, small peaks into the future. It was their spiritual gift. This was one of those times, and she said so. "I had a dream you got your baby." She was a little nervous about explaining this was no typical dream.

"Really? We are going to get a call from the adoption agency?" My mom was excited. Adoption had been on everyone's mind for the last months. It was exciting to think that a baby would be added to the family in the next year. "Is it a girl or a boy?"

"It is a girl. And it is twins." Grandma Ileen said.

"Twins?" She paused. That is a nice dream, *Lynda thought.*

"Yes, two baby girls. I saw them."

They drove on. It would be exciting when a baby came. It was fun to imagine a happy day. Twins, though?

My mom and grandmother drove on and continued a few hours shopping. They put the conversation behind them as they laughed and enjoyed a day together. They were soon home and walking into the house. My dad, Allen, was sitting on a chair, nervous and excited. They could tell something had happened.

"I just got off the phone with the Children's Home Society!" he said, still holding back information. He jumped up to share the news. "They just called, and you'll never believe it! Our baby is already here. It is a girl. Not just one, it is twin girls!"

My grandmother sat down with a thunk. My mom looked over, and she was visibly shaken and holding her hands to her chest. "I saw them! Those are our babies!"

Chapter 10

GATHERING

Allegory of the Tame and Wild Olive Tree

The prophet Jacob in the Book of Mormon tells the allegory of the olive tree. In the single longest chapter, he recounts a story from the brass plates, as told by the Prophet Zenos. In Jacob 5, the Lord teaches the Nephites, and us, a significant set of truths about the gathering of Israel.

Allegories are stories. They are stories that have a lot of really long, extended metaphors. A modern example of allegory is C.S. Lewis's *The Lion, the Witch, and the Wardrobe.* It is filled with Christian symbols like the Christlike Aslan suffering and dying on a sacrificial altar to redeem Edmund. Its symbolic nature has layers of meaning. The strength of allegory is its effectiveness. It is much more engaging to read a story than a set of directives. My favorite parts of the Old Testament are the emotional stories of its characters, like Jacob and Esau or Leah and Rachel. I rarely sit down and excitedly open up the Ten Commandments or a list of Levitical priestly requirements. "Thou shalt not" and "a priest shall not make himself unclean" do not catch my emotion. A story, especially one that makes me feel and engage like an allegory, captures the mood, context, and meaning. Thus, allegory is a powerful teaching tool.

The prophet Zenos uses allegory to explain the scattering and gathering of Israel, as well as the many different twists and turns that people will take throughout history to scatter and gather. It is complex, and that's what makes it exciting. The trick is understanding some of the basic symbols.

As the allegory of the tame and wild olive tree is about the gathering of Israel, let's look at just nine verses to see if we can't unlock some of its profound insights. Before you read it, here are a few clues.

Olive branches are people. Tame olive branches are the covenant people, as the tribes of Israel. Being "tame" or "wild" is a way of describing their covenant faithfulness. Wild = unrighteous, decay, and apostasy; tame = righteousness, covenant-making, and faith. All the actions of working in a vineyard like digging and pruning are the work of the Church. Things like missionary work, ministering, teaching, and preaching are a few examples of "digging and pruning." That is probably an oversimplification. But with those few ideas in mind, let's read a few verses.

> 60 And because that I have preserved the natural branches
> and the roots thereof, and that I have grafted in the natural
> branches again into their mother tree, and have preserved
> the roots of their mother tree, that, perhaps, the trees of my
> vineyard may bring forth again good fruit; and that I may
> have joy again in the fruit of my vineyard, and, perhaps, that
> I may rejoice exceedingly that I have preserved the roots and
> the branches of the first fruit—
>
> 61 Wherefore, go to, and call servants, that we may labor
> diligently with our might in the vineyard, that we may
> prepare the way, that I may bring forth again the natural
> fruit, which natural fruit is good and the most precious
> above all other fruit. 62 Wherefore, let us go to and labor
> with our might this last time, for behold the end draweth
> nigh, and this is for the last time that I shall prune my
> vineyard.
>
> 63 Graft in the branches; begin at the last that they may be
> first, and that the first may be last, and dig about the trees,
> both old and young, the first and the last; and the last and
> the first, that all may be nourished once again for the last
> time.

> 64 Wherefore, dig about them, and prune them, and dung
> them once more, for the last time, for the end draweth nigh.
> And if it be so that these last grafts shall grow, and bring
> forth the natural fruit, then shall ye prepare the way for
> them, that they may grow.
>
> 65 And as they begin to grow ye shall clear away the branches
> which bring forth bitter fruit, according to the strength of
> the good and the size thereof; and ye shall not clear away the
> bad thereof all at once, lest the roots thereof should be too
> strong for the graft, and the graft thereof shall perish, and I
> lose the trees of my vineyard.
>
> 66 For it grieveth me that I should lose the trees of my
> vineyard; wherefore ye shall clear away the bad according as
> the good shall grow, that the root and the top may be equal
> in strength, until the good shall overcome the bad, and the
> bad be hewn down and cast into the fire, that they cumber
> not the ground of my vineyard; and thus will I sweep away
> the bad out of my vineyard.
>
> 67 And the branches of the natural tree will I graft in again
> into the natural tree; 68 And the branches of the natural tree
> will I graft into the natural branches of the tree; and thus
> will I bring them together again, that they shall bring forth
> the natural fruit, and they shall be one.
>
> Jacob 5: 60—68

I love this allegory section because I see my own family in it. I have been sharing some stories of my family, birth, and adoption. It is miraculous to see how the Lord has worked to bring my families' different branches and roots together. There are many ways the allegory can apply to my family and yours. The story may speak to people you know now, like a sibling or a child. Or perhaps, the allegory is speaking to you about your ancestors who have passed on.

Ponder a few of the ideas presented in the Allegory and see if the Spirit doesn't speak to you about the scattering and gathering happening in your own life.

Grafting and Planting

Grafting and planting are signs of the Lord's love for all His children, the scattered and the gathered. He can use his covenant few to save the roots, the mother tree, and the lost family members. In addition, the grafting of wild branches into the tame olive tree represents the conversion of those who become part of the Lord's covenant people. Those who are the roots or are grafted are all part of the tree.

Roots

Roots: individuals who the Lord has covenanted with anciently, like Abraham and Sarah. Roots may also represent the Lord's covenants with those who follow Him.

Lord of the Vineyard

Who is speaking in these verses? Who is the Lord of the Vineyard, and who are the servants? If you are a servant, what are you being asked to do? What special gifts do you have that can help build the kingdom?

An Aside: Olive Tree, Grafted Together

When Lisa and I were adopted, we became part of a new family. We needed them, and they needed us. I have roots and branches of my "olive tree," for which I am grateful. I am honored by my roots, my birth family. I am thankful for their love and their courage. I am thankful for making it possible for me to be born at this time.

I am also eternally thankful for my adopted family's "faithful branches." Sealed together for time and all eternity, we are bound together in the Lord. They were willing to take a risk, reach out to another, and open their homes and hearts to two tiny babies. My parents have made me who I am. They have loved me and supported me. My brothers are everything a kid could want. My brothers are protectors, exemplars, and advisors. My family showed me unconditional love and acceptance. They encouraged me and taught me the gospel of Jesus Christ. In every action, they exemplified Him, even in accepting two little foundling twins.

They accepted us completely. We are family. They are ours, and we are theirs, forever.

I needed them as much as they needed me. And I think that is how the Lord works. As much as we need, He provides. As much as we give, we receive blessings back tenfold. The Master says it this way, "For whosoever will save his life shall lose it: and whosoever will lose his life for my sake shall find it" (Matt 16:25). When we empty ourselves, giving everything we have to the Savior, we find our true selves. Despite everything we offer, we receive more than we could ever imagine.

Both of my families are important, and I see the hand of God in every action.

As it says in Jacob 5:68 (formatting added):

> And the branches of the natural tree will I graft into the natural branches of the tree;
> and thus will I bring them together again,
> that they shall bring forth the natural fruit,
> and they shall be one.

Captain Moroni

There is a story that we often tell of an amazing man, reminding us of our covenants. The story is also a story about the remnant.

The political situation was dangerous and fragile: "and thus were the affairs of the people of Nephi exceedingly precarious and dangerous" (Alma 46:7). Many in and out of the church had been persuaded by the "flattering words of Amalickiah . . . [and] dissented even from the church." It was a dangerous, politically volatile time. The society and spirituality of the nation were in flux. During such a time, when the people were living the church and politically unsure, what did someone do?

A hero stepped up. Moroni, a chief commander of the armies, recognizes what is happening. He puts on his armor, and tears off a piece of his coat, a remnant, and writes,

> In memory of our God, our religion and our freedom, and our peace, our wives, and our children—and he fastened

> it upon the end of a pole. . . . and he took the pole, which had on the end thereof his rent coat, (and he called it the title of liberty) and he bowed himself to the earth, and he prayed mightily until his God for the blessings of liberty to rest upon his brethren, so long as there should be a band of Christians remain to possess the land.
>
> Alma 46:12–13

The people follow Captain Moroni and make a solemn covenant to protect the people's freedom. They promise to obey their covenants. And then, Captain Moroni reminds them of one more critical element,

> Yea, let us preserve our liberty as a remnant of Joseph; yea, let us remember the words of Jacob, before his death, for behold, he saw that a part of the remnant of the coat of Joseph was preserved and had not decayed. And he said—Even as this remnant of garment of my son hath been preserved, so shall a remnant of the seed of my son be preserved by the hand of God, and taken unto himself, while the remainder of the seed of Joseph shall perish, even as a remnant of this garment. Now behold, this giveth my south sorrow; nevertheless, my soul hath joy in my son, because of that part of his seed which shall be taken unto God.
>
> Alma 46:24–25

Jacob prophesied that a portion of Joseph's family would be a remnant. The Lord would save that remnant. Captain Moroni reminds the people *who they are* and the promises they have from the Lord. He makes a symbolic flag, a remnant of his coat, to remind them that they are a remnant.

Key Ideas to Remember

- The Book of Mormon is sacred scripture that teaches over and over that the Lord remembers His remnant.
- The allegory of the tame and wild olive tree teaches many lessons of the Lords' plans to save us.

- We are a remnant of Joseph, and the Lord will preserve us. As we remember Him, we will be preserved.
- As a remnant of Joseph, we are tasked with the gathering of Israel.

Chapter 11

O THAT I WERE *an* ANGEL

Mission Call

The day I received my mission call was one of the most exciting days of my entire life. I lived in Salt Lake at the time, working in a laboratory and going to school at the University of Utah. My family lived in Southern California, my twin was attending BYU, and I lived in a shared apartment near Salt Lake City. I had been waiting for a few weeks to receive my call. It was a couple of weeks late, by my count. Living in Utah, I knew that I would receive it on a Thursday if my call was extended and placed in the mail. I had not received it last week, nor the week before. I was getting very anxious.

My excitement was at its peak: "Would it come today? Where would I serve?" I imagined all the places that I could go. Perhaps I would go to Japan like my oldest brother, Mike. He was a genius, so learning Japanese was easy. I wasn't sure an Asian language would be very easy for me, but that seemed exotic. Maybe I would be called to Brazil like my brother Rick. He had so many stories of teaching people, learning from them and their unique cultures. One of my prized possessions was a soccer jersey he had brought back. I could see myself walking down the cobblestone streets of rural Brazil. The possibilities seemed endless, and I daydreamed about all the foreign places I could go.

I had just turned twenty-one, so I was just eligible to go on a mission for the Lord. The age is slightly younger now, but at twenty-one, I had lived away from my parents' home for a few years. I was not very nervous about being on my own—it was an adventure. I also could serve the Lord. I felt ready to serve, brave to go far from home, and excited to share the gospel. One thing I didn't want to admit, at least not out loud, was that there were a few places I did not want to go. I did not want to serve in Salt Lake or anywhere close to home. That meant if it was in the Southwestern United States or Utah, I would have served but been disappointed.

I know I am not supposed to think that and should love whomever I serve, but I imagined myself opening my call and it is saying, "Utah, Bountiful," and me pretending to be excited (sorry, Bountiful—you're great, but I already was living in Salt Lake City, and it didn't sound very exciting). Hey, I had my focus on the wrong thing. I admit it now. I was more interested in something exotic than the people and Lord I would serve. So, as I anxiously awaited my call, imagining all the places I could go to, I also imagined all the places I would be a little disappointed about.

Finally, it was the fourth Thursday since I had turned in my paperwork, and I was sure my oversized envelope with a mission call, signed by the prophet himself, would be in my mailbox. I got off work early so I could be there when the mail arrived. I drove home from work, rushed to the mailbox, opened it, and it was there! The envelope from the Church headquarters was addressed to me. I knew this was the moment I had been waiting for. I hurried into the house. No one was home. I called my parent's house to open it with them on the phone. No answer. I tried over and over again. I called my twin's apartment—also no answer. It was the middle of the afternoon when most were working or at school.

Today it is common for people to post that they have their call and will be opening that evening, live, so all could participate. I could have waited until my friends and roommates got home from work. I also could have waited until I could call family on the phone. But I'm going to be honest here. That was never going to happen. I have always been independent and impatient. So, right there in the middle of my apartment living room, I opened my mission call by myself. I pulled the packet of paper folded in half from its envelope. I unfolded the papers and started to read as fast as my eyes could go. I had been called on a mission to serve the Lord. I was called to the Barcelona, Spain mission, speaking Spanish for eighteen months.

I stood there, stunned. It was real. I was going to Spain. And I was disappointed.

I know that I was supposed to be honored to go where the Lord called. But standing there with the paper in my hand with a Spanish-speaking mission call, I was disenchanted. I'm embarrassed to admit it now. A few months from opening my call, I would be serving the people. I would be filled with a deep love for the Spanish and Catalan people. Through long hours of prayer and service, I learned that I loved my mission and the people of Spain.

At that moment, I was disappointed with the mission call in hand, reading Spain. It felt close to home. As I had grown up very near the Mexico-United States border in San Diego, speaking Spanish was commonplace. More people spoke Spanish than English at my high school. Until that moment, I had not realized that I had foolishly thought this was like serving in my hometown. I was disappointed because it was not exotic. I am embarrassed to say it now, but I was young and foolish then.

I put on a brave face and acted excited. I was. That's not fair—I was very excited overall. I had prepared my whole life, and now it was here. I knew I would learn to love the people I had served.

I had been called to gather the one. "If it so be that you should labor all your days . . . and bring . . . one soul unto me, how great shall be your joy" (Doctrine and Covenants 18:15).

When we think of the gathering of Israel, we think of formal missionary work. We are all called to serve formally or informally in our lives. It is an honor and a privilege to be called to serve the Lord in this way. There are also many stories of missions and missionaries in the scriptures. The sons of Mosiah, Samuel the Lamanite, Nephi and Lehi, and many others grace the pages of ancient scripture. Modern scripture records the callings of many modern missionaries. Our calling is to be a messenger, a missionary, to the world.

It can be a challenge at times to share our testimonies of the Savior. We may not know how to start or be unclear about who to talk to. We might not even feel we have the skills required to teach and preach. Or, like one young and foolish missionary (me!), we may feel like our calling is not what we were expecting. Yet the redeeming hope and love that fills our souls when we recall our redemption can help us find courage. With the power of the Spirit, we can share what has changed in our own hearts with those around us.

The Prayer of Alma the Younger

The prophet Alma the Younger is beloved. After failing to hear the teaching of his parents, Alma had been "seeking to destroy the church of God" (Alma 36:6). His conversion to missionary, high priest, and prophet is dramatic and inspirational. His change shows the power of the Atonement of Jesus Christ in the life of anyone who turns their heart to the Lord. The power of Jesus Christ to redeem us is truly a miracle.

We have talked about the power of poetry to evoke emotion. The Old Testament is not the only book of scripture with strong emotion. The Book of Mormon also has poetry that invites us to feel the power of the prophet Alma. After an angel calls him to repentance, Alma changes. He speaks of the power of Christ's redemption: "And oh, what joy, and what marvelous light I did behold; yea, my soul was filled with joy as exceeding as was my pain!" (Alma 36:20). It is this powerful grace that Alma wishes to share with others.

Alma has a prayer, perhaps a poem that shares his deepest desires to share the gospel with others. He cries out to be able to share the change that Jesus Christ has offered him. His greatest desire is to share the gospel. We are privileged to peer into Alma the Younger's soul. There we hear his deepest wish to bring others to Christ.

[1] O that I were an angel, and could have the wish of mine heart,
that I might go forth and speak with the trump of God,
with a voice to shake the earth,
and cry repentance unto every people!

[2] Yea, I would declare unto every soul,
as with the voice of thunder,
repentance and the plan of redemption,
that they should repent and come unto our God,
that there might not be more sorrow upon all the face of the earth.

3 But behold, I am a man,
and do sin in my wish;
for I ought to be content with the things
which the Lord hath allotted unto me.

4 I ought not to harrow up in my desires the firm decree of a
just God,
for I know that he granteth unto men according to their
desire,
whether it be unto death or unto life;
yea, I know that he allotteth unto men,
yea, decreeth unto them decrees which are unalterable,
according to their wills,
whether they be unto salvation or unto destruction.

5 Yea, and I know that good and evil have come before all
men;
he that knoweth not good from evil is blameless;
but he that knoweth good and evil,
to him it is given according to his desires,
whether he desireth good or evil, life or death, joy or remorse
of conscience.

6 Now, seeing that I know these things,
why should I desire more than to perform the work
    to which I have been called?
7 Why should I desire that I were an angel,
    that I could speak unto all the ends of the earth?

8 For behold, the Lord doth grant unto all nations,
of their own nation and tongue,
to teach his word, yea, in wisdom,
all that he seeth fit that they should have;
therefore we see that the Lord doth counsel in wisdom,
according to that which is just and true.

9 I know that which the Lord hath commanded me,
and I glory in it.
I do not glory of myself,

but I glory in that which the Lord hath commanded me;
yea, and this is my glory,
that perhaps I may be an instrument in the hands of God
to bring some soul to repentance;
and this is my joy.

10 And behold, when I see many of my brethren truly penitent
and coming to the Lord their God,
then is my soul filled with joy;
then do I remember what the Lord has done for me,
yea, even that he hath heard my prayer;
yea, then do I remember his merciful arm which he extended towards me.
11 Yea, and I also remember the captivity of my fathers;
for I surely do know that the Lord did deliver them out of bondage,
and by this did establish his church
yea, the Lord God, the God of Abraham, the God of Isaac, and the God of Jacob,
did deliver them out of bondage.

12 Yea, I have always remembered the captivity of my fathers;
and that same God who delivered them out of the hands of the Egyptians
did deliver them out of bondage.

13 Yea, and that same God did establish his church among them;
yea, and that same God hath called me by a holy calling,
to preach the word unto this people,
and hath given me much success,
in the which my joy is full.

14 But I do not joy in my own success alone,
but my joy is more full because of the success of my brethren,
who have been up to the land of Nephi.
15 Behold, they have labored exceedingly, and have brought

forth much fruit;
and how great shall be their reward!

16 Now, when I think of the success of these my brethren my soul is carried away,
even to the separation of it from the body,
as it were, so great is my joy.

17 And now may God grant unto these, my brethren,
that they may sit down in the kingdom of God;
yea, and also all those who are the fruit of their labors
that they may go no more out,
but that they may praise him forever.
And may God grant that it may be done according to my words,
even as I have spoken.

Amen.

Alma 29, formatting added

Key Ideas to Remember

- The Lord calls all of us to share His gospel with others.
- When we share the gospel, we offer salvation to others.
- A call to serve has been extended to all of us.
- Alma the Younger's prayer reminds us of the power the Savior offers to help us fulfill our calling to help gather scattered Israel.
- When we remember the love and grace the Savior has given us, we "speak with a voice to shake the earth."

Chapter 12

BRING THEM HERE *to* ME

The Mission Field

I got to the Mission Training Center full of excitement. It did not take long to throw myself into the work. I loved the language training, the discipline and structure, and especially learning how to teach the gospel of Jesus Christ. My training district was small, and we grew close.

Something changed in me. I stopped thinking so much of myself. I spent long hours memorizing Spanish and how to teach. I especially loved throwing myself in the scriptures, principally spending time with the Book of Mormon. Reading and studying it with such purpose seared itself into my soul. I began thinking about I could not wait to get to Spain! All of my foolish thoughts about it being too prosaic vanished. Soon it was time to get to Barcelona.

I arrived in Barcelona full of the Spirit of missionary work. I talked to everyone. I remember yammering on about gospel ideas with my first taxi drive from the Barcelona airport. I can only imagine how bad my Spanish was, but my heart was in it.

While I was in my first area, I met Dolores. Lola, as her friends called her, was an elegant woman. She lived along the Segre river in Lleida, Spain. In a beautiful home overlooking the river, she lived alone. She was a widow, her children grown and moved to their own homes, she was eager to learn the gospel. She was distinguished, cultured, and dignified, making me self-conscious. My Spanish was far from perfect, and I only spoke a few words in Catalan, her primary language. I felt more like a goofy kid than an ambassador of the gospel.

Lola invited us over week after week to hear about the gospel. She asked deep questions about the authority of baptism, what was required of her to enter a covenant, and what was genuine faith in Jesus Christ. She was very earnest and intent. After our lessons, she would offer us lunch, always with complete place settings, sumptuous dishes, and refined European delicacies.

One afternoon, my companion and I got caught in a rainstorm. We were soaked. We realized we were only a few blocks from Lola's house, cold, wet, and far from home. We went by to see if we could dry off. She graciously welcomed us in, got us dried off, warmed up, and dressed in her clothes. I had never worn a business suit of such quality before. I felt like a Spanish banker, ready to make a business deal. Lola was always giving, always prepared, and she was a bit intimidating for a young missionary.

During our next lesson, she shared some tragic news and why she was learning about the gospel. She had cancer. It had progressed enough that she wasn't sure she would survive. Dolores was anxious to learn all she could about the Savior in the time she had left.

The news was devastating to my companion and me. I immediately felt inadequate. How would I, just a young woman speaking a language that wasn't my own, be able to teach her? I was already intimidated by her social status, manners, and elegance. Now, I felt the burden of her salvation as well. Knowing that she may die soon made everything seem more intense as if every word I said needed to have meaning. I was overwhelmed and distressed with the responsibility. I wrote to my dad back home, expressing that I didn't think I could do it. In a week, I got his letter back.

"Lori, you're enough. The Lord put you there, at this time, for a reason. Whatever gifts you have, that's what Lola needs. No one can do the work alone. Let the Savior do the heavy lifting."

Feeding the 5,000

There is a story of a miracle in the middle of the Lord's mortal ministry. Jesus feeds five thousand with just a few loaves of bread and a couple of fish. We learn about Jesus's power to create in a few short verses. He is incredible and can make bread and fish to feed thousands. He is compassionate to give the people, far from town, the food so they are not hungry. The Lord is kind and thoughtful. Those are all insights about the Savior. There is also another lesson about the gathering of Israel and what He expects of us.

> 13 Now when Jesus heard this, he withdrew from there in
> a boat to a deserted place by himself. But when the crowds
> heard it, they followed him on foot from the towns. 14 When
> he went ashore, he saw a great crowd; and he had compassion
> for them and cured their sick.
>
> 15 When it was evening, the disciples came to him and
> said, "This is a deserted place, and the hour is now late; send
> the crowds away so that they may go into the villages and
> buy food for themselves."
>
> 16 Jesus said to them, "They need not go away; you give
> them something to eat."
>
> 17 They replied, "We have nothing here but five loaves
> and two fish."
>
> 18 And he said, "Bring them here to me." 19 Then he
> ordered the crowds to sit down on the grass. Taking the five
> loaves and the two fish, he looked up to heaven, and blessed
> and broke the loaves, and gave them to the disciples, and the
> disciples gave them to the crowds.
>
> 20 And all ate and were filled; and they took up what was
> left over of the broken pieces, twelve baskets full. 21 And
> those who ate were about five thousand men, besides women
> and children.
>
> 22 Immediately he made the disciples get into the boat
> and go on ahead to the other side, while he dismissed the
> crowds. 23 And after he had dismissed the crowds, he went
> up the mountain by himself to pray. When evening came, he
> was there alone.
>
> Matthew 14:13–22, NRSV

When we read this story, it is easy to be overwhelmed with the size of the miracle. Jesus is the Christ, able to create food and feed thousands. That is a remarkable element of the story. It is worthy of study and reflection. But two elements can teach of about our role.

Context

When we jump into a block of scripture verses, we don't always get the setup before. We start reading and may miss what was happening before. The context is critical to learning something key about the Savior's nature in this story.

Before this pericope, we read that John the Baptist had been killed in the verses. We don't have those verses quoted here, but the news the Lord is receiving is that King Herod had murdered John. The Lord's reaction is telling. When the disciples hear the news that John had been killed, the Lord immediately stops to mourn. "Now when Jesus heard this, he withdrew from there in a boat to a deserted place by himself" (verse 13). He gets in a boat to get away and pray. Why would the news of John's death be disturbing?

John was a close relative of Jesus. Mary and Elizabeth, Jesus and John's mothers, had both been together during their pregnancies, sharing in the joint miracles of the two boys. John was the prophet who prepared the Savior's way (Isaiah 40:3, Malachi 3:1, 1 Nephi 10:7–10). He baptized the Savior (Matt 3:13–17) and taught the people repentance, baptism, and the coming of the kingdom of God (John 3:23–24). We could say John was more than just a family member in some ways. John was Jesus's mission companion. John prepared the way, taught and preached, and was one of the few who understood the mission of the Savior. The death of John, His friend, His relative, and His companion in the work of the gathering was terrible news. It was distressing, disturbing, and upsetting. Jesus needed some time alone.

He gets in a boat and travels across the Sea of Galilee and goes to a remote place to have some time to Himself. And the people that He had been teaching and healing? They follow Him. We can only imagine some of the thoughts the disciples were having. Why wouldn't the people just give Him a minute to mourn? They were insistent and demanding, and He could use some time to process and pray. It would be normal to expect that the Savior would ask for some private time.

Yet, ever compassionate, He stops, teaches, heals, and then shows us a few more important lessons.

At the end of the verses, you see the Lord retreats alone, to get the time He needed to mourn and pray for John: "And after he had dismissed the crowds, he went up the mountain by himself to pray. When evening came, he was there alone" (verse 23). This episode demonstrates His example to give and serve first before taking time to Himself. He shows us that when we are hurting and need help, perhaps one way we can be like Him is to serve another. We are like Him when we turn in service in our time of need. We can find solace and support in reaching out to others. We can help gather Israel by being like Him.

Being like Him

The disciples have a central role in this story. We see that they help Jesus try and get away from the crowds when He needs some time. They also help him teach. Imagine yourself there. You have been following the Master and learning from him. It has been a year or more into His ministry, and you're starting to think more like Him. As you notice, the people are far from town. And these are sick, hurting people. It is late, and they do not have food far from anywhere. Thinking more like the Savior, you are beginning to notice what He would see. In this case, you notice that the people need food.

You approach the Savior: "Jesus, the people need to leave soon. They don't have food, and they need to find some in the surrounding towns." The Lord tells you something surprising.

Jesus said to them, "They need not go away; you give them something to eat" (verse 16).

"We have nothing here but five loaves and two fish," you reply. (verse 17). You only have a little bit you brought for the disciples and the Lord. You cannot possibly feed everyone with that little bit. It is barely enough for you.

And here is where the Lord teaches us something magnificent and encouraging to the gathering of Israel. He tells them, "And he said, 'Bring them here to me'" (verse 18). It as is if He is saying, "Bring what you have, that's perfect! That's exactly what I need."

The Lord can take whatever we have, whatever small meager, tiny offering, and make it enough. Like taking the few loaves and couple of fishes, He makes them enough. As disciples, as we enter His service, Jesus Christ takes what we bring and makes it more. He says to us, "that's perfect. That's exactly what I need." Then he blesses it and makes it something miraculous.

As a disciple of the Master, whatever we bring to him is enough. We are enough. We bring our singing skills or musical abilities to him, and it is perfect. We offer our ability to connect with friends and neighbors, offer friendship and hope, and make it more. We deliver our talents with administration, numbers, and organization, and he magnifies it in the kingdom. We consecrate ourselves, our broken, imperfect, and incomplete selves, to the work, and He says, "It is exactly what I need!" and He makes it so.

We offer to Him our meager offerings, and He reminds us, "Bring them here to me."

Key Ideas to Remember

- The mission of the gathering of Israel can seem daunting.
- When we are struggling, service can bring joy.
- The Lord has given us talents and asks, "Bring them here to me."
- Whatever we bring to the Lord, He can make it more.
- The Lord can bless our offerings and make them miraculous.

Chapter 13

GATHERING *the* OUTSIDER

Outcast

"We don't want you!" The car drove by that night with a young man shouting from the window.

I was in Northern Spain, it was late, and my companion and I were almost home from a long day of meetings and trying to teach people the gospel of Jesus Christ. The hourly schedule is different in Spain, with the day's big meal, mediodia *lasting three or four hours in the middle of the day. So, to follow Spanish custom, we were home in the afternoon for those hours and worked later into the evening, like everyone else. It was summer, the evening contacting was finishing up. We were walking home in the late evening.*

I heard the car screech past, barely registering with the man was saying. He was shouting at us to go home. We had not been particularly welcomed in this town. As the home of the Jesuits, a Catholic order, it was a bastion of tradition. The young man hanging out of the car window shouted at us as missionaries. It was just another reminder that many did not want us here.

Suddenly, out of nowhere, I felt a sharp pain in my chest. I was confused. I could not quite figure out what was going on. Was I having a heart attack? I put my hand up to feel my heart, and it came away covered in something. In the light of the overhead streetlight, I could see my hand was covered in mustard. I didn't have a heart attack. In an instant, I understood what had happened. The pain I had felt was food the passing car and hurled my way, striking my square in the chest. I had been pelted with a sandwich.

Tears leaked out of my eyes. I wasn't very physically hurt, but I was emotionally and spiritually injured. It had been challenging to try to share the gospel of Jesus Christ, only to be yelled at, mocked, and now, pelted with sandwich parts. I trudged home, my head hanging down as I tried to hide my tears. My faithful friend and companion picked up the remains of the baguette sandwich and hurled it back into the street in solidarity.

I knew that being a missionary would be challenging. Still, I was unprepared for the lack of acceptance, and even the meanness, that happened to us as missionaries. The scripture stories are full of many persecuted teachers, and I realized I was not alone. And while I had had many, many wonderful experiences with the Spanish people, this was not a unique occurrence. We had been yelled at, had rocks thrown at us, and even my companion's skirt had been lit on fire with fireworks. Being stoned with a sandwich was just one more event in a list of messages we had received from our neighbors.

I was an outsider, and it was clear, at least to some, I was unwelcome.

The Savior's Mission to the One

The Savior came to save all of us. When we think of the gathering of Israel, it is easy to think of the house of Israel. We may think of a people group like the tribe of Judah. Perhaps we think of a civilization like the Nephites. Indeed, much of the Old Testament and the Book of Mormon talk in the big picture. They discuss entire people groups. We hear about "the Israelites" or the "Nephites" and "Lamanites." While individuals' key accounts, the ancient prophets speak to large groups. Jonah was called to teach the entire city of Nineveh, the capital of Assyria. King Benjamin spoke to all his people, teaching and preaching from a tower so all could hear him. Thus, it is easy to think of the gospel being taught to entire cities. When the Savior came to His mortal ministry, He frequently changed lives one by one.

He quoted scripture when he stood up in the synagogue to proclaim His ministry.

> 16 And he came to Nazareth, where he had been brought up: and, as his custom was, he went into the synagogue on the sabbath day, and stood up for to read.
>
> 17 And there was delivered unto him the book of the prophet Esaias. And when he had opened the book, he found the place where it was written,
>
> 18 The Spirit of the Lord is upon me, because he hath anointed me to preach the gospel to the poor; he hath sent me to heal the brokenhearted, to preach deliverance to the captives, and recovering of sight to the blind, to set at liberty them that are bruised,
>
> 19 To preach the acceptable year of the Lord.
>
> 20 And he closed the book, and he gave it again to the minister, and sat down. And the eyes of all them that were in the synagogue were fastened on him.
>
> 21 And he began to say unto them, This day is this scripture fulfilled in your ears.
>
> 22 And all bare him witness, and wondered at the gracious words which proceeded out of his mouth
>
> Luke 4:16–22

The Lord came to reach out to all people. He came to work with the poor, the sick, and the spiritually outcast. He came to rescue the one. As we consider the gathering, we should consider reaching out to those in need.

It is encouraging that when the Lord announced His arrival, He talked about teaching the poor, healing the sick, freeing the prisoner, and healing the brokenhearted. By contrast, He did not announce the destruction of cities the deposing of Kings. Rather than change the world from the outside, He came to cure it from the inside.

He came to save us, one by one.

The Mission of the Church of Jesus Christ

The mission of the Church of Jesus Christ of Latter-day Saints is "to help all of God's children come to Jesus Christ through learning about His gospel, making and keeping promises with God (covenants), and practicing Christlike love and service ."* As members of His Church, we practice Christlike love, and helping others is part of our mission.

The Savior's earthy mission is full of examples of teaching the one. He meets people where they are, most often those that society has left behind. He talks to tax collectors, rebels, and sex workers. He meets with the sick, the deaf, and the blind. He touches and heals lepers.

We covenant to reach out to those around us when we are baptized. We promise to be "willing to mourn with those that mourn; yea, and comfort those that stand in need of comfort, and to stand as witnesses of God at all times and in all things" (Mosiah 18:8). The Savior has taught us how to gather Israel—one by one.

Each teaching of the Savior is a lesson in the gathering of Israel. He teaches us how to live and how to be more like Him. He also teaches us how to reach the individual, even when that person is ourselves. There are two remarkable stories, examples of how we can help gather Israel. In these two scriptural stories, we can see ourselves as those who can help teach and serve others. We can see ourselves in the outcast, the unwanted, and the unclean. In the examples of the Savior, we can learn how we can gather the one.

The Leper

According to Matthew, after Jesus teaches the Sermon on the Mount in the gospel, there is this strange story. As the Lord descends from the Mount, we find a hidden gem of gospel truths. It is just four verses long, and so, if we don't stop and pause, we'll miss it. After the greatest of sermons ever given, the Lord practices what He has been preaching and shows us perfectly how to gather the one. He exemplifies reaching out to the sick, the separated, the alone, and the outcast.

---

* "The Church of Jesus Christ of Latter-day Saints," information page on church website, https://www.churchofjesuschrist.org/learn/about-us?lang=eng. Last updated 18 November 2021.

> When he was come down from the mountain, great multitudes followed him. And, behold, there came a leper and worshipped him, saying, Lord, if thou wilt, thou canst make me clean.
>
> And Jesus put forth his hand, and touched him, saying, I will; be thou clean. And immediately, his leprosy was cleansed. And Jesus saith unto him, See thou tell no man; but go thy way, shew thyself to the priest, and offer the gift that Moses commanded, for a testimony unto them.
>
> Matthew 8:1–4

The story is brief. After teaching the sermon, Jesus encounters a leper. The leper asks him something profound, "Lord, if thou wilt, thou canst make me clean." Jesus says that he does will it and touches the man, and he is cleansed. The now-clean-leper is commanded to perform the sacrifice the Law of Moses required, showing himself to the priest, ending his leprosy, and keeping the whole thing a secret. That's it. The Savior's ministry and mission are summed up in just a few short verses.

But that's just it. It is so short and wrapped in a unique context that it is easy to miss. Maybe because we are so familiar with hearing about leprosy in our scripture study, we blow right by it. Or perhaps we just think, "the man was sick and healed," so the story is one of healing. It is a powerful and beautiful miracle, but does it stand out?

There are two parts of the story that stand out. This story has become one of my favorites because right here, encapsulated, is Jesus's whole message to us and the world. First, let's talk about being a leper.

Unclean and Leprosy

When the Savior approaches the leper, the leper asks for something unique. He asks to be made clean. Clean? That's an odd way to tell the first miracle of Jesus in this gospel. Why not, "Forgive my sins?" "Heal my wounds" or "Save me!" But . . . clean? Why is Matthew's first miracle story one about spiritual cleanliness? The idea of cleanliness goes back to the holiness code in the Old Testament.

Holiness

We use the word holy often in church settings. We read about things being holy, like the temple. Right on the outside of the temples is the phrase "Holiness to the Lord." That exact phrase is embossed on the breastplate of Aaron, who was the high priest of the tabernacle. Outside of scripture and the temple, it is not a word we use very much. The Lord is holy. The word holy is separate and unique. It means to be set apart, dedicated, and consecrated to a higher purpose. When Isaiah has a vision of God in the temple, the seraphim surrounding the Throne cry out, "Holy, holy, holy" (Isaiah 6:3). Hebrew doesn't have a superlative form of comparison. In Hebrew, you cannot say pure-est at the end of a word to make it the "most." You cannot say "holiest" or "best," so you repeat a word to make it more extreme. The divine beings surrounding the throne tell us that God is the most holy, the holiest, the highest-most-holy-one.* They tell us that the divine is incorruptible, beyond death and decay. He is pure and undefiled.

The Old Testament is heavy with these ideas. Specifically, the rules and regulations about what is holy and how to return to holiness are called the holiness code. It sets apart the physical and spiritual nature of this unique nature. Leviticus is about that separateness, that holiness. It details the structures, clothing, and rituals that are to be maintained or are required to return to this holy state.

For example, Aaron wears a breastplate when he ministers in the temple engraved with "Holiness to the Lord" (Exodus 28:36). Here is a crucial idea: God is Holy, so to draw closer to Him, we must become holy, too. Aaron wears the phrase on is chest, nearest his heart, reminding him that his very self must be completely pure. He must be holy with his heart and mind. As a priest of God, he must consecrate his heart to God. The tabernacle and temple were places where heaven and earth would meet, an area set aside where the Lord can dwell. Holiness is a state of separateness, set apart and without corruption. Thus, the tabernacle, and later the temple, was set up in concentric circles of increasing holiness. The clothing, materials, and rituals testified of God's separate nature and His Holiness.

---

* M. C. Lyons, "Holiness," ed. John D. Barry et al., *The Lexham Bible Dictionary* (Bellingham, WA: Lexham Press, 2016).

Another Key idea: God's holiness is something we cannot survive alone. We must become more like Him to get close to His holy presence. We need the power of the Savior, His Grace, to become holy enough to be like our Father in Heaven. I think of it like the sun. If we get too close without protection, we will burn up. Like the sun, God's power and holiness are so mighty that we cannot get too close without holiness.

Unclean

The term the scriptures use to talk about being un-holy is "unclean." A few things make us unclean if you lived in Ancient Israel. You could be unclean both ritually and morally. We use the word "clean" the same way. You could say your shirt is unclean, or you have "a clean conscience." The majority of references in the Old Testament refer to ritual uncleanliness. The prophets start using the idea of ritual uncleanliness to explain moral uncleanliness.

Ritual uncleanliness happened during everyday life. You became unclean, having been in contact with a dead person, having skin that looks flaky and dead, and some exposure to certain bodily fluids. To be clean, we must be far from death. A word you'll sometimes see used for this type of uncleanliness is corruption. When something is dying or dead, it starts to decay, fall apart, and return to dust. Things that were evidence of decay and death, such as touching a dead body or having flaky, leprous skin, meant you were unclean. Also, ordinary human experiences, like childbirth, or contact with certain bodily fluids, could make us unclean.

Whether ritually or morally unclean, we would have to follow the proper procedure to be clean again. Typically, this involved waiting for a short time, washing, and participating in a sacrifice. Then, we were clean again.

In the Savior's mortal ministry days, the purity rituals had become burdensome and overreaching. The Lord encourages us to be clean, not just ceremonially, but in our hearts (Matthew 15:3–20). While ritual purity is less familiar to us today, the question of purity was a critical issue for the Jews in Christ's day.

Being Unclean

Being unclean in Ancient Israel was tough. Being in this state had consequences. First, it meant that you had to be separated from others. For some, this just meant that you had to put temple practice on hold for a while, and others had to be apart from other people for days or weeks. For us today, this may not seem like a big deal. For many, a few days apart would not have been risky. But there were times where being apart from home, the family, the tribe meant you were in grave danger. If you were a leper, you could never get clean until you were healed of the disease. For some, this meant a lifetime of separation. Let me say that again, for some. This meant a lifetime of separation.

Imagine the loneliness. Without family, without friends, apart from everyone you know. You had no human contact, no touch, no hug. There was no one to be near, no one to protect you, no kind hand to reach out during your saddest days. Being a leper meant you could not be near other people. For some, a short-term skin malady would quickly pass, and you could return to the company of your family and friends. However, for a leper, your condition might be permanent. You were "outcast, unclean."

That's the context of the leper. His story, his miracle, is set within the greater context of the Sermon on the Mount. It is here that we learn what the Savior's healing means.

The Sermon on the Mount

The Savior's message on the Mount is a call to a higher and holier way. Taking many of the commandments, he asks us to go deeper. Rather than just obedience, he asks us to change our hearts. "You have heard it said," he repeats over and over, recalling the law and the commandments. "Ye have heard it said of them of old time, Thou shalt not kill; and whosoever shall kill shall be in danger of the judgment: But I say unto you, that whosoever is angry with his brother . . . shall be in danger of the judgment" (Matt 5:21–22). Jesus is teaching us that we have to change inside, too. Following Him, learning to be more holy, is about changing how we feel and act on the inside. Holiness, approaching God, is about changing our hearts, and He is there to show us the way.

It is this moment, as he is descending the Mount, after teaching us how to become holy, that he meets the unclean leper.

We Are the Leper

It may be hard to put ourselves in the story. Understanding what it was like to be a leper is something we may not be familiar with. By putting ourselves into the heart of the leper, we learn more about the love of the Savior

Imagine living your life apart from everyone that you know and love. You are covered in sores, your skin burns, and itches. You have tried everything to get rid of it—creams, lotions, washing—and nothing helps. It has been a long time since you have felt the touch of another person. No hugs, no simple touches on the shoulder. You haven't had a family dinner, chat with a friend or even a job. You are alone.

You have heard about Jesus of Nazareth. He is gathering crowds and followers. He is teaching something new and exciting. It is even said he is a healer. Hanging back because of your leprosy, you have listened to his sermon. You have felt something you have never hoped to hear. You know this man is something special. Some are even saying He is the Messiah. You wait, rushing to where he'll be, coming down the hillside.

What if He can heal you? What if He can make you clean?

The Savior Comes Down the Mountain

The Savior finishes teaching His great sermon. A sermon in which He teaches us the true meaning of the law and commandments shows us the application in one action. He sees a lone leper, and where others move away, He moves toward him.

In the leper, we see ourselves. We are broken, sinful, and separated from the Lord. We long to be welcomed back onto His embrace, come home again, and be clean and forgiven. The Lord taught, just moments before, the Way is more than just the right actions. It is changing our hearts.

And this is the second principle that makes this story so impactful to me. The concept of the Holiness code teaches us more about ourselves, not to tell us how different we are but how much the divine wants to welcome us back into His presence. He creates a special place where the incorruptible One can share a little of the Divine with His children. Holiness isn't a prohibition as much as an invitation. The Lord reaches out to the fallen, the corrupt, and the disgraced.

Holy Again

Since the garden and the Fall, the physical separation is real from God. The spiritual separation is just as absolute. All of us are separate and desperate for the life of God's presence. How do we get there? How do we become holy or gain this grace of Christ? How can we be gathered in?

We come to Christ. In humility, we allow Him to make us more than we could ever make of ourselves. "My grace is sufficient for all men that humble themselves before me; for if they humble themselves before me, and have faith in me, then will I make weak things become strong unto them" (Ether 12:27).

> If ye shall deny yourselves of all ungodliness, and love God with all your might, mind and strength, then is his grace sufficient for you, that by his grace ye may be perfect in Christ.
>
> Moroni 10:32

The gospel is not for perfect people. Instead, the good news is that the Savior reaches out to gather the broken, sick, and lost. He came down from the Mount and embraced the leper, who longs to be welcomed back like us.

"Make me clean." The leper, who is unnamed so we can relate and see ourselves in him, needs to be welcomed back into the human family again. Being a leper, being unclean, he is forbidden to live in the town, prohibited the touch of another, separate, apart, alone. With one phrase, the leper is all of us, crying out, "Let me be part of the human family again, and be touched and close to others. Let me live like a regular person and enjoy a meal, a touch, a hug." And like the leper, we spiritually want to return to God. We cry out to Christ, "Let me come into Your presence. Let me be part of Your family again, and be in Your embrace. Make me clean."

We are all separated, fallen, yet desperate to be back. We ask just to be physically healed but to be embraced. We ask to be seen, loved, and welcomed home. We ask for more than just physical healing but to have the separation and the differences removed. We long to be welcomed back into the presence of our Father. We long for the moment when we will encounter the Savior of the world, when we too will fall to our knees in front of Him and cry out, "Make me clean."

Key Ideas to Remember

- We can all feel like outsiders.
- The Lord's message is for all. We can help bring others to Christ as we remember His atoning sacrifice.
- We help gather Israel when we return to Him.

Chapter 14

A REMNANT *of the* KINDRED SHALL RETURN

Eventually, my time in Spain was complete, and I was called home. It was tough for me to leave behind the people. Despite a few challenges, I had grown up spiritually there. I grew up in Barcelona. I left a part of my heart in Barcelona. I wept when I had to go. These were my people. They had accepted me, too. They were mine, and I was theirs.

After returning to San Diego, I saved up some money, worked for Paul Duncan, my old seminary teacher, and eventually returned to the University of Utah, where I had attended school before I left. My life returned to the rhythm of work and school. About a year after returning, I got a call from my twin, Lisa.

"I found her! I found our birth mom!" Lisa had been married a short time and was expecting their first child. She wanted to know more about our birth parents' medical history to be prepared for the baby. Perhaps there were medical issues that she should know about and prepare for. She reached out to the Children's Home Society to get a copy of our file. While our adoption was officially closed, and no information could be shared with any of the parties, some details about medical history could be given. She called and requested those. Eventually, after some red tape, a social worker called her with the surprising news. "There is a letter in here from your birth mom. The letter was fairly recent and said she would like to

meet you." Lisa was shocked and amazed. Of course we would want that letter.

The state of California has a lot of laws. Many were to protect the birth family, the foster family, and my family in a closed adoption. So even though a letter from our birth mom was recent and gave her contact information and her desire to meet, we had to follow the regulations. Both parties had to fill out and notarize various release documents. This was not hard for Lisa. The social worker had to find our birth mom again, make contact, and initiate the proper forms. This all took time, much of it behind the scenes. It was hard to know the status of all the documents. The social worker, who only worked at Children's Home Society once a week, had to move slowly and precisely. She had many rules and regulations, forms, and filings to follow the law.

Our birth mom did not know we had been adopted together. Instead of me filling out and approving all the same forms, we were advised to let that news be the first information shared once our phone numbers were exchanged. The paperwork social worker contacts seemed to suspend time. That lasted only a few weeks. That felt like forever.

Finally, the day arrived when Lisa and Gloria had filled out all their paperwork, and phone numbers were exchanged. At this point, we knew virtually nothing about one another. We did not even know each other's names. As twins, Gloria did not know if we were adopted together or separately. And while Gloria had given us names at birth, they were changed by our adopted parents. Lisa and I didn't even know those full names, only that we were once Desiree and Dawn, now Lisa and Lori. We had tiny scraps of information about each other. But in moments, we would meet, and the mysteries would start to be revealed.

It is almost always positive when adopted kids and birth families meet in popular media. The adopted children feel some need to find their roots, and the birth parents have been striving to find and be part of their birth children's lives. At some point, there is a happy reunion where all parties embrace, tears are shed, and everyone's life is complete. Reality can be a lot different.

Every adoption story is different. Adoption has affected so many lives, and my story is only my own. I can only share my story, how it changed me and my siblings and parents. If my adoption story is different from yours, I understand. My story is probably different than even my twin's.

Also, I want to pause here to explain my parents. My parents, Allen and Lynda Denning are wonderful. I never felt like I needed to "find myself" or that I was abandoned. I knew my birth parents were teenagers when we were born, and growing up sealed to my family as a Denning was a dream. I loved my family, brothers, and parents, but to be very clear, my parents are fantastic, and I am blessed to have them. I was meant to be with them. If finding my birth parents hurt them in any way, I would never have done it. With their unfailing support and love, they were as curious as we were to find this part of my past.

So, despite feeling accepted and loved, I was deeply curious about my birth parents. And here, while I waited by my phone for the call from my birth mom, a million thoughts buzzed through my head. What was she like? Would she be like me? Would she be proud of me? I would talk to a person intimately connected to me in minutes, yet whom I knew nothing about.

Feelings and relationships are infinitely complex. We do not even have words or definitions of some of the relationships I'm describing. I use terms like "birth family" and "adopted family" to represent the complex associations. It's those moments before the phone rang, the complexity, the roil of emotions, hanging suspended, unable to fully be expressed. Just like the names we keep inventing, I didn't have words for what was happening. Was it excitement or anticipation? Fear or dread? Hope or wonder? There weren't words to tell of this. In a few minutes, all my imagination would be replaced with reality. Time paused.

Eventually, the phone rang.

Woman of Samaria

As Jesus begins his ministry in the gospel of John, he takes a trip through Samaria and has some of the first success with a group of outsiders. In John, some of the first people to recognize Jesus as the Messiah are the gospel of Jesus Christ is for all people, even people who are different, separate from the group, and unwanted. The story of the women of Samaria is about gathering in all people.

When we pick up the story, we may not see how politically charged this story would have been. This story would have been shocking and unexpected and would have stirred up controversy. Jesus, leaving the area of Judea, travels North through Samaria.

> 3 He left Judæa, and departed again into Galilee. 4 And he
> must needs go through Samaria.
> 5 Then cometh he to a city of Samaria, which is called
> Sychar, near to the parcel of ground that Jacob gave to his
> son Joseph.
>
> 6 Now Jacob's well was there. Jesus therefore, being wearied
> with his journey, sat thus on the well: and it was about the
> sixth hour. 7 There cometh a woman of Samaria to draw
> water: Jesus saith unto her, Give me to drink. 8 (For his
> disciples were gone away unto the city to buy meat.)
> 9 Then saith the woman of Samaria unto him, How is
> it that thou, being a Jew, askest drink of me, which am a
> woman of Samaria? for the Jews have no dealings with the
> Samaritans.
> 10 Jesus answered and said unto her, If thou knewest
> the gift of God, and who it is that saith to thee, Give me to
> drink; thou wouldest have asked of him, and he would have
> given thee living water.
> 11 The woman saith unto him, Sir, thou hast nothing to
> draw with, and the well is deep: from whence then hast thou
> that living water? 12 Art thou greater than our father Jacob,
> which gave us the well, and drank thereof himself, and his
> children, and his cattle?
> 13 Jesus answered and said unto her, Whosoever drinketh
> of this water shall thirst again: 14 But whosoever drinketh
> of the water that I shall give him shall never thirst; but the
> water that I shall give him shall be in him a well of water
> into everlasting life.
> 15 The woman saith unto him, Sir, give me this water,
> that I thirst not, neither come hither to draw.
> 16 Jesus saith unto her, Go, call thy husband, and come
> hither.
> 17 The woman answered and said, I have no husband.
> Jesus said unto her, Thou hast well said, I have no husband:

18 For thou hast had five husbands; and he whom thou now hast is not thy husband: in that saidst thou truly.

19 The woman saith unto him, Sir, I perceive that thou art a prophet. 20 Our fathers worshipped in this mountain; and ye say, that in Jerusalem is the place where men ought to worship.

21 Jesus saith unto her, Woman, believe me, the hour cometh, when ye shall neither in this mountain, nor yet at Jerusalem, worship the Father. 22 Ye worship ye know not what: we know what we worship: for salvation is of the Jews. 23 But the hour cometh, and now is, when the true worshippers shall worship the Father in spirit and in truth: for the Father seeketh such to worship him. 24 God is a Spirit: and they that worship him must worship him in spirit and in truth.

25 The woman saith unto him, I know that Messias cometh, which is called Christ: when he is come, he will tell us all things.

26 Jesus saith unto her, I that speak unto thee am he.

27 And upon this came his disciples, and marvelled that he talked with the woman: yet no man said, What seekest thou? or, Why talkest thou with her?

28 The woman then left her waterpot, and went her way into the city, and saith to the men, 29 Come, see a man, which told me all things that ever I did: is not this the Christ? . . . 39 And many of the Samaritans of that city believed on him for the saying of the woman, which testified, He told me all that ever I did.

40 So when the Samaritans were come unto him, they besought him that he would tarry with them: and he abode there two days. 41 And many more believed because of his own word;

42 And said unto the woman, Now we believe, not because of thy saying: for we have heard him ourselves, and know that this is indeed the Christ, the Saviour of the world.

John 4:1–29, 39–42, formatting added

History of the Samaritans

The history of the Samaritans is scant and sometimes contradictory. Samaria was the ancient capital of the ten tribes, the Northern tribes, the Northern Kingdom. Some claimed to have continued living in the North as descendants of the tribes of Ephraim and Manasseh. Despite the Assyrian conquest, some claimed only a portion had been carried off. Those carried off are what we call the "lost ten tribes." Those that were left behind continued to see themselves as Israelites. Others claimed that no real Israelites were left behind. Instead, the people who took over those lands were from surrounding areas (2 Kings 17:24). Whether they were the remnants of Ephraim and Manasseh or new people who had inhabited the land, they called themselves Samaritans.*

In the years before Jesus's time, some of the tribe of Judah are allowed to return from exile to Jerusalem and rebuild the temple. (This is the story of Ezra and Nehemiah if you want to brush up on events.) Ezra 4 tells the story that when the Judahites (in Jesus's time known as Jews) returned, the Samaritans were excited to help rebuild the temple. While the Judahites started to rebuild the temple, some Samaritans came to help and were rebuffed, turned away, and refused.† Their beliefs made them unworthy in the eyes of the returning Jews. The Samaritans, rejected, started to sabotage the project (Ezra 4:4–5, 24) and the wall that protected and surrounded the city. (Ezra 4:17–23). They also believed that proper worship should be on Mount Gerizim, not Jerusalem.

These social and political factors will come into play in the Lord's discussion with the Samaritan woman at the well. They'll talk about the position of Samaritans and Jews and their animosity toward each other (See also John 4; Luke 9:51–3; Matt 10:5–6). They'll discuss the

---

* John J. Pilch, *A Cultural Handbook to the Bible* (William B. Eerdmans Publishing Company: Grand Rapids, MI; Cambridge, U.K., 2012), 73.

† Brian Maiers, "Samaritans," ed. John D. Barry et al., *The Lexham Bible Dictionary* (Bellingham, WA: Lexham Press, 2016).

religious differences, worshiping on different "mountains," meaning Jerusalem or Gerizim.‡

Context about Samaria

The woman of Samaria is distinctive for two more reasons. First, she is a woman. For a Jewish man to be talking to a woman alone would have been uncommon. Outcast may be the wrong word. In this case, she was separated from, removed, and different. Because of her gender, it would have been inappropriate for her to talk to a man alone. It would have been improper for her to learn from a teacher. It would have been wrong for her to speak alone to Jesus.

Secondly, she is distinctive socially from her town. The clue to this is the time of day that this event is happening. It is somewhere about noon. The disciples went to find something to eat. It feels like the middle of the day, like lunchtime. Women don't draw water at noon typically but early and later in the day, when it is cooler. Women also tend to travel together for safety (Exodus 2:16). Thus, at the well, by herself at noon, a woman means she is unpopular. In the story, we hear why. Her relationships have made her unwelcome.

Social Outcast

The Lord has this strange interruption in the middle of the conversation. After discussing water, the Lord speaking metaphorically, and the woman thinking literally, He tells her to call her husband. Let's look at it again because it is crucial.

> **15** The woman saith unto him, Sir, give me this water, that I thirst not, neither come hither to draw.
>
> **16** Jesus saith unto her, Go, call thy husband, and come hither.

Strange right? In the middle of teaching about the Savior's role as the source of all life, physical and spiritual, He tells her to get her

‡ John C. Johnson, "Mishnah," ed. John D. Barry et al., *The Lexham Bible Dictionary* (Bellingham, WA: Lexham Press, 2016).

husband. Doesn't that seem like odd timing? It is for us, but for Him, it is not.

He reveals that she has been married five times and lives with another man. This shocking news is what has made her a social outcast. The people of her town have not well received her inappropriate relationships. She is shocked that He knows the information and calls Him a prophet.

There are two levels of this fact that teach us about the Savior. First, He is not shocked, hurt, or dismissive of the woman for her choices. While she is a social pariah because of her multiple marriages and living situation, the Lord still talks to her. What a beautiful truth. The Lord still loves us and will welcome us, regardless of our actions. He engages with the woman, and us, in whatever spiritual state we are in. We do not need to wait to be better to approach Him. We can begin the disciple's journey today, wherever we are. He already knows our situation, our sin, and He loves and welcomes us back. He will forgive us and teach us, despite whatever we have done.

Second, marriage is a common symbol of the Lord's covenant with the tribes of Israel. The symbolism of the Bride being the Church and Bridegroom being the Lord starts in the garden and continues to the book of Revelation. The Lord calls himself the husband to the house of Israel. "For I am married unto you" (Jeremiah 3:14). "I was an husband unto them" (Jeremiah 31:32). Also, "For thy Maker is thine husband" (Isaiah 54:5). The Apostle Paul understood the metaphor calling Christ the husband of the Church (Ephesians 5:23). The Lord loves us as closely as the groom loves his spouse.

The bond of the covenant Christ has with the Church is similarly binding as a marriage covenant. As Jesus Christ is the Bridegroom, the house of Israel is the bride. "I sware unto thee, an entered into a covenant with thee . . . and thou becamest mine" (Ezekiel 16:8). The Lord has bound Himself to us, as covenant Israel in a relationship as close and loving as marriage. We, the Church, and Israel, He will remember and redeem.

When the woman of Samaria meets the Lord, He immediately lands on the idea of a covenant marriage. If the woman had been married many times and is living with another, she could be representative of Israel, going after other gods. When we forget our covenants to

Him, we are unfaithful spouses. The house of Israel had been scattered for so long. They had forgotten their covenants. Rather than being a non-sequitur, the Lord recalls her situation and the covenant situation of the Northern tribes. Both are lost. They have lost their way, fallen off the path, and the Lord will gather them in. Like us, the Israelites longed to be gathered back into the arms of the Bridegroom.

Setting

One more feature, the setting, is essential in the story. Once again, ancient scripture is a bit different and uses different techniques to tell the story. Explaining a location is another example.

In modern histories or even a conference talk, we take time to explain the setting, history, and location of the event. We may give background information and tell the history of the place or who owned it in the past. We also explain all-important past events in our setting in our historical recounting. In modern movies, the technique is often a musical montage, quickly showing all the events that happened in the past. In the space of one song, we watch the history, the historical setting, and why things are happening there.

Pardon the fictional example. The movie "Up" begins with a marriage montage.* In five short minutes, we see the married life of Carl and Ellie. It sets the story, the characters, and even their home setting. It shows them saving to travel to South America, but setbacks and life get in the way. These elements, including the scene of their home and the South American dream trip, are critical to the story's main thrust. (If you have not seen the movie, it is worth watching. Just be sure and bring tissues—it's a tear-jerker.)

Ancient scripture does not have movie montages. The setting is often a single location, like a well, that is linked to other stories. We are expected to have all the many stories of the well, specifically Jacob's well, preloaded in our memories. Thus, when that one indication tells us that Jesus is meeting a Samaritan woman in the middle of the day at Jacob's well, we recall all past events. That description,

---

* *Up*, dir. Peter Doctor (2009, Walt Disney Studios Motion Pictures).

that one indication of setting—where something takes place—is our scriptural equivalent of a music montage.

Jacob's Well

Jacob is the great Patriarch of the book of Genesis. His grandfather is Abraham, who receives and restores the new and everlasting covenant to the world. His father, Isaac, in return, gets the blessing and covenant. And Jacob receives the blessing and covenant promises after Isaac. These stories comprise Genesis's second half and the zoomed in view (see Genesis 12–33). Jacob, the covenant son and Patriarch, camps near a well outside Shechem when he returns from exile (Genesis 33:1–20). Jacob had fallen out with his twin brother, Esau, decades ago. Jacob had received the covenant while Esau, the older son, and the traditional recipient, had not. Esau had vowed to kill Jacob. Jacob, now married with eleven sons, had returned to Canaan. After wrestling with an Angel of the Lord, a more mature man, Jacob, had just received a new covenant name (Genesis 32:22–31). As the culminating event of this story, Jacob builds a well and an altar and names it, "God is the God in Israel" (Genesis 33:20). Thus, Jacob builds a well in a story of God's covenant love and faithfulness in keeping His promises.

Thus, Jacob's well is the story of the covenant. The promises of the covenant are the promises offered to all humanity. A well also sparks another association—marriage. In a day when there was a division of labor by gender, women often worked at the well. They collected the water in the morning and the evening for the family and animals. We are reminded of Rebekah meeting Abraham's servant at a well, as the servant was on a holy mission to find Isaac a bride (Genesis 24). Jacob met his wife Rachel at a well (Genesis 29:1–11). Moses also meets his wife, Zipporah, at a well, defending her and her sisters from ruffians. When we think of wells, we should think of the bride and the bridegroom and marriage covenant. Then, a well recalls a close relationship, a divine covenant, and faithfulness.

New beginnings and revelations also happen at wells and water. Hagar, when cast out with Ishmael, is out of water. There, "And God opened her eyes, and she saw a well of water, and she went, and filled the bottle with water, and gave the lad drink (Genesis 21:19). Salvation, reconciliation, life, and covenant are all wrapped up in the setting of a well.

It is with these concepts in mind that Jesus meets the Samaritan woman. Who is the Samaritan woman? She is a social outcast three times over. She is a woman, she is a Samaritan, and she is not well-liked in her town. Yet, He teaches her that He is the Living Water. He reminds her and us of the covenant faithfulness of the Lord. He will not forget us. And it is to her, the outcast, just as to us, that the Savior is Messiah. Christ, the Savior of the World, reveals himself to the least. He reveals Himself as the long-awaited Messiah in our moment of need, "I that speak unto thee am he."

The Message

The Savior visits people who are enemies of the Jews. Upon going into Sychar and the region of Samaria, he meets and talks to a woman who is the least of her town and an outcast among her people. He reaches out and reveals Himself as the Son of David, the King, and Messiah. He could have revealed Himself to kings and queens, the priests of the temple. Instead, He changes one heart and one mind. He chooses a person who needs the "good news" most in their lives, welcomes her back into the fold, and gathers His flock. The house of Israel was gathered then, as it is today.

Key Ideas to Remember

- The Savior's offer of salvation is available to everyone.
- The mission of the Church of Jesus Christ is to help all come to Him.
- We can feel separated from God, like a leper, but we are made clean through the Savior's atoning sacrifice. We can offer this blessing to others as we exemplify Him.
- We become Christlike, exemplifying His holiness and changing our hearts.
- The Lord will gather in all of His family. We are a part of this gathering in our families, associations, and call to be holy.

Chapter 15

GRAFTED BACK IN

The Call

Riiiiing.

The phone was ringing. On the other end was my birth mother. In just a few minutes, all of the mystery would be resolved.

Riiiing.

What would she be like? Would she be like me? Would I be like her? I sat there, nervous, excited, not sure what to think.

Riiiing.

After weeks of paperwork, notaries, and official documents, Lisa had gotten word that the social worker was shortly giving her Gloria's phone number. Just minutes ago, Lisa had gotten the phone number, and they were talking. We decided not to do a conference call but to call one at a time, to meet each other separately.

Riiiing.

I had so many emotions. I didn't know what kind of emotions they were. I had never experienced meeting a birth parent before. Was I supposed to be excited or nervous? In popular culture, adopted children always had some hole in their life they needed to be filled. And their adopted parent was pining away from them. And only together could they be complete.

Riiiiing.

I did not feel like that. While everyone's feelings and adoption story are unique, mine was not about filling some emptiness in my psyche.

Yet, when I examined my emotions, they were confusingly complex. They roiled around in my heart, never resolving. Being adopted was part of my identity, but it did not define me. It was my beginning, but it was not my ending. Would meeting Gloria change my direction?

What was I waiting for? When I answered the phone, I would be no different than before I picked it up. All of my experiences, brothers, sister, and dearest parents—none of those things would change. I would meet this person, and I would still be Lori.

I answered. "Hello. This is Lori."

And we talked. Gloria was kind, respectful, and nervous. For the first twenty minutes, we shared the basics. Lisa and Gloria had talked before my call, and so we covered some of their earlier conversations. She had not known that Lisa and I were adopted together and were surprised to find out we were together. It wasn't common for twins to be kept together, so she wondered. As the social worker had reached out, she could not say that I was there, too, waiting to be connected. It was all a happy surprise.

She learned our names, not the ones she gave us. She shared details about her growing up, the story of her pregnancy, and our birth. She also told us of the middle names she had given us. I was not just Dawn, but Dawn Michelle. Lisa was Desiree Marie. Gloria was embarrassed to say Marie was her middle name, and she didn't want it to be too presumptuous that she gave Lisa her name.

It was all surreal. It felt like any conversation you'd have with a new friend—everyone on their best behavior, and no one saying much. While we swapped the basic details of our lives, my emotions were confusing. It was like I was watching anyone else have a conversation.

We talked for an hour or so. She was charming and kind. I was goofy and talkative.

After a while, Gloria asked, "Have you been happy? Has your life been . . . okay?" She was worried that we had not been loved. Finally, we came to our greatest hopes and fears. She was afraid that I would hate her or feel abandoned.

"I have had a perfect life. My parents are awesome. My brothers, well, despite their teasing, are loving and fun. And having a twin was the built-in friend every kid hopes for." I paused. I knew what she feared that I would hate her. In a flash of realization, I knew what she truly wanted to know.

"Thank you. Thank you for giving me life. Thank you for letting me go to my family. My life has been blessed. I am where I am supposed to be."

Isaiah's Sons

The Lord loves us and plans the best for all of us. As we are bound in covenant love, He will help us be gathered in, return to Him, and be blessed. He calls us back into the fold, welcomes our repentance, and restores our blessing. Gathering can happen in many ways, like the individual Samaritan woman and the leper. He also restores brothers, sisters, and families.

The prophet Isaiah speaks of children, revealing critical elements of the gathering of Israel. Isaiah's prophecies are profound. The Lord says, "great are the words of Isaiah" (3 Nephi 23:1). The prophet taught in a time when the Northern tribes were being scattered and the Southern tribes were under great political upheaval. He is a prophet during the tumultuous time of the scattering. Thus, his teachings are some of the most profound for understanding the gathering of Israel. He teaches of these events, both scattering and gathering, using symbols.

Isaiah's teachings and prophecies have layered meaning and application. Isaiah lists three sons whose names are uniquely prophetic. We have already learned that names have symbolic significance. Recalling that, we look to the meaning of the various sons of whom Isaiah prophesies.

First, we're most aware of Isaiah 7:14: "Therefore the Lord himself shall give you a sign; Behold, a virgin shall conceive, and bear a son, and shall call his name Immanuel." Matthew indicates this prophecy fulfilled in Jesus Christ in Matthew 1:23. Thus Immanuel—God with Us—is a prophetic revelation of Jesus as the Son of God. An angel reveals the fact to Nephi: "And the angel said unto me: Behold the Lamb of God, yea, even the Son of the Eternal Father!" (1 Nephi 11:21).

Isaiah has his own sons with prophetic names. Both sons' names have a bearing on the gathering of Israel. The first son, whose name is especially catchy, is Maher-shalal-hash-baz (Isaiah 8:1, 3–4). The meaning of the name is "speedy spoil, hasty plunder."* The prophet encouraged the Southern Kingdom of Judah not to fear the Assyrians. The politics of the time are a bit complex, but Isaiah advised the people to have faith in the Lord. The Lord gave Isaiah the name to remind us that the Lord can provide guidance and protection even from worldly kingdoms.

Isaiah has a second son whose name also has symbolic meaning for the gathering of Israel: *Shearjashub*, "A remnant shall return" (Isaiah 7:3).† The Lord gives Isaiah and his wife the prophetess, a son whose name gives us hope for the future of the house of Israel.

> [20] On that day the remnant of Israel and the survivors of
> the house of Jacob will no more lean on the one who struck
> them, but will lean on the Lord, the Holy One of Israel, in
> truth. [21] A remnant will return, the remnant of Jacob, to
> the mighty God. [22] For though your people Israel were like
> the sand of the sea, only a remnant of them will return.
> Destruction is decreed, overflowing with righteousness.
> [23] For the Lord God of hosts will make a full end, as decreed,
> in all the earth.
>
> Isaiah 10:20–23, NRSV

The Lord uses the names of Isaiah and the prophetess's sons to teach us about the scattering and gathering. First, we learn the name of a special child, Immanuel, who is the world's Savior. Then, Isaiah's sons remind us, first, to trust in the Lord during times of conflict. Finally, the Lord reminds us that a remnant will return when we are scattered and lost. It is up to us if we want to be a part of that remnant.

The Lord's mission has always been salvation. The Father loves us and has provided a Savior to help us return. The message of the gathering, of salvation, is found in the prophets. It is even woven into the names of the prophet's children. The message of redemption is in the story of twins.

---

* John D. Barry et al., eds., "Maher-Shalal-Hash-Baz, Son of Isaiah," *The Lexham Bible Dictionary* (Bellingham, WA: Lexham Press, 2016).

† Barry et al., "Shear-Jashub, Son of Isaiah."

Twins

A story of twins in the Bible has always been my favorite. The story of Jacob and Esau is the story of brothers. It is also a story of the covenant, redemption, and blessing. We have already touched on this story numerous times. However, we have always looked at it from Jacob's point of view from the blessed son. As we examine the idea of grafting back in, we reflect on those who are on the outside. Perhaps they have been overlooked, or perhaps they have left the covenant path for a time. What blessings does the Lord have for those branches? Now, it is time to examine Esau.

Esau is the older brother. When he is born, it is said he is red and hair. Esau means "hairy."‡ His nature characterizes him. He is a man of passions, almost animalistic. He spends his time outdoors and is an accomplished hunter like an animal. Covered in hair, we are reminded of this nature. Esau's association with red reinforces this idea. He is born red, and later, his descendants are called Edomites, meaning red. Later, when he sells his birthright for stew, it is "red pottage" (Genesis 25:29–30, KJV 1900 Authorized Version).§ His association with red recalls a passionate man. He follows his instincts.

It isn't only his skills at hunting and physical description that give us insights into his personality. Esau is a man of passion. He is also married twice over, outside the covenant (Genesis 26:34–45, 28:8–9). He sells his birthright for stew. From his physical description of being red and hairy to hunting, selling your birthright for food, and marrying, these associations tell us something about Esau. He has drive, is emotional, and goes after what he wants. Esau adores his father, and Isaac loves him deeply in return. He is also a man of passion. He is complex.

He is just like us.

Esau seems like the "bad guy" in the story. Typically, there are no totally good or totally bad people in scripture. To differing degrees, they are people, and they all have failings and successes. Esau is like

‡ Walter A. Elwell and Barry J. Beitzel, "Esau," *Baker Encyclopedia of the Bible* (Grand Rapids, MI: Baker Book House, 1988), 715.

§ *The Holy Bible: King James Version*, Electronic Edition of the 1900 Authorized Version. (Bellingham, WA: Logos Research Systems, Inc., 2009), Genesis 25:30.

all of us when we let our passions and desires rule over us. We are like an animal, thinking only of our instincts. We may marry for love or passion or for other reasons. They may even be good reasons, but we make decisions apart from those the Lord would have us make. We may not value our covenants or the blessings of the gospel. And that sounds a lot like all of us from time to time. We let our desires and passions rule us.

When Jacob receives the blessing of the birthright, Esau is so upset he wants to kill Jacob. "And Esau hated Jacob because of the blessing wherewith his father blessed him; and Esau said in his heart, The days of mourning for my father are at hand; then will I slay my brother Jacob" (Genesis 27:41). Jacob believes it and flees. Jacob stays away for decades.

The story of Jacob and Esau follows Jacob for the following chapters of Genesis. We don't know much of what Esau is doing. We do not know if he matures, changes his mind, or how he develops. We only know that when Jacob and his family are going to return, Jacob is very fearful of Esau. Jacob sends lavish gifts ahead of his arrival in hopes of softening any leftover resentment Esau may feel (Genesis 32:5–6). Jacob's messengers return to report that Esau is coming with four hundred men. Jacob is mortified. He splits up his family into two groups, so if Esau intends to destroy, at least some will survive (Genesis 32:7–8). Jacob prays, begging for the Lord's divine protection, even invoking the promises of the covenant (verses 9–12).

Imagine for a moment. Jacob is traveling home with his family. He has his wives, servants, herds, and even little children. To split your family into two groups because you fear reprisal is scary. Jacob pleads with the Lord to protect him and his family from Esau's wrath. It speaks to the real fear Jacob has. This feels really intense, and it may not end well.

And Esau? We know he is coming to meet Jacob after decades apart. He is bringing a small army. Will this be the same "red" Esau?

Then, the brothers reunite.

Esau

As Jacob crosses over the river, he looks up and sees his brother approaching. Surrounded by four hundred men, Jacob approaches Esau.

And there, for a moment, we pause. Anything could happen. The tension builds. The two brothers stand apart. Esau is on one side with hundreds of men. Jacob is, on the other, with his family, including children. For a long moment, no one moves. Then, slowly, Jacob approaches.

Jacob bows down to the earth in front of his brother. Not once, not twice, but seven times. Each time he bows, he steps a little closer to Esau.

Bow.

Step.

Bow.

Step.

Then, Esau runs to meet Jacob.

Esau embraces his brother, pulling him in, and hugs him tight into an embrace. Tears stream down his cheeks and fall on Jacob's neck.

Jacob, hugging him in return, weeps.

Joy overwhelms them all. In an instant, all the fear is gone. Esau and Jacob introduce their families. Esau gives back all the gifts Jacob had sent. Esau has grown. He has been blessed with prosperity, just like Jacob. They are no longer young men struggling over the birthright but brothers who share and bless each other. Jacob insists that Esau take the presents. After all, Jacob has seen the face of God.

They part as friends. They part as brothers.

Esau's Redemption

Esau is no longer the young man led by his passions. He is a gracious and loving brother. Grown and matured, Esau has changed. There is one more story about Esau we haven't told yet. It may be the key to understanding Esau's redemption.

When Jacob received the birthright, Esau had been out hunting for Isaac, his father. Isaac dearly loved Esau and wanted to bless him. Jacob knew Esau wasn't worthy of the covenant birthright, but Isaac loved him (Genesis 25:28). Isaac sent Esau to hunt and bring back a favorite meal, and then Isaac would bless Esau. While Esau was hunting, Jacob and Rebekah contrived to gain the birthright (see Genesis 27). Jacob covers himself in a goatskin to emulate Esau's hairy nature. He disguises his voice and brings in a meal. Isaac, now blind, blesses Jacob in Esau's stead.

Jacob is scarcely out of the tent from receiving his blessing when Esau returns.

"Let my father arise, and eat of his son's venison, that thy soul may bless me."

And Isaac trembled exceedingly and said, "Who?"

Isaac now realizes what has happened. It was Jacob whom he had blessed just moments ago. Isaac works through everything aloud, saying, "Where is he that hath taken the venison, and brought it to me, and I have eaten of all before thou camest, and have blessed him? Yea, and he shall be blessed."

And Esau heard his father's words, he cried with a great and exceedingly bitter cry and said, "Father, bless me, even me also, O my father."

Esau then, with terrible realization, understands what Jacob has done. It is then that we hear the anguish in Esau.

"Has thou not reserved a blessing for me?" He weeps. He pleads with his father, "bless me, even me, too. O, my father."

Jacob does bless Esau with great blessings. Yet, the birthright, the covenant promises did not go to Esau. Isaac realizes now that Esau wasn't worthy. He seals the blessing on Jacob (see Genesis 27–28:4).

A Blessing for Me?

Was this a turning point for Esau? We have had moments where we are brought to our knees in despair. When we realize that we have lost the Lord's blessing by our own mistakes or by the world's challenges, we reach out and exclaim, "Bless me, even me also, O my Father."

It is at that point that we can change. The Lord will once again embrace us and draw us close. We can receive a blessing. The path is never so far or the sin so great that the Lord does not welcome us back. We can choose to repent, change, and return to our covenants. Lord did bless Esau, and He will bless us. When we fall to our knees, He will support and embrace us when we realize we need Him. Then, when we have returned to Him, we become new people. The Lord will bless us when we return. We can be grafted back in.

Esau took this moment to change. The Esau who embraces Jacob is the redeemed man, the brave soul who chooses the Lord.

Key Ideas to Remember

- The Lord will welcome back all those who have wandered.
- He will restore our blessings when we return.
- It takes bravery and strength to return to the Lord.
- The Lord loves all His children.

Chapter 16

GATHERING A REMNANT

After meeting my birth family, mainly my birth mom's family, it was fun to learn of our unique heritage. Lisa and I learned we had a solid Mexican heritage from the Sonora region of Mexico. Gloria looked Hispanic. Lisa and I must take after our birth dad and his Swedish heritage, as we don't look very Hispanic.

Learning about Gloria's family was fascinating. It was also a little surreal. It was like hearing a story about someone else. It felt like they were people I should know and relate to, but I did not know them. I loved hearing about Grandma Ramona and the history of the family. Gloria often talked of her mom, Ramona, who had died just a few years before. Since I spoke Spanish, it would have been great to talk to her in Spanish. We missed meeting her in person by just a few years. The family spoke of Ramona's incredible beauty. One night I was talking to my Aunt Carol. Although she was the youngest of Ramona's daughters, Carol was Gloria's older sister from her first marriage.

Carol had been a nurse and in her young twenties when Lisa and I were born. When the family learned of Gloria's pregnancy, they sent her from the central California area to San Diego to have the baby away from rumors and prying eyes. Gloria was, after all, just a teenager. And that was in a time when having a baby out of marriage was heavily frowned upon. Carol, as a nurse, was the perfect person to care for Gloria and her baby. At this time, no one knew Gloria was expecting twins.

Carol cared for Gloria, gave her prenatal care, and was a motherly influence. Although only twenty-two, Carol made plans for the birth, even considering how to buy a house and help raise the baby. Ultimately, she decided she could not support her sister and a baby alone. Carol shared all of this information on the phone with me one night, telling me details about our birth, her role, and all the events surrounding those days.

Carol was also the family historian. She graciously spent hours telling me about each of her siblings—my aunts and uncles. She also told me of her mother, my grandmother Ramona. Ramona was a beautiful woman, and some of her best features were her dark hair framed against her white, white skin.

"I thought Ramona was from Mexico," I said. I realized that Mexico had a lot of ethnic diversity, yet this information intrigued me.

"Oh, her mother, Beatrice, was. She was from Sonora. But her father, Vicente Duran, was from Barcelona, Spain."

I think I dropped the phone. My birth mother's maternal grandfather was from Barcelona, Spain.

I had served my mission in Barcelona, Spain.

My family was from Barcelona, Spain.

> And after the house of Israel should be scattered they should be gathered together again; or, in fine, after the Gentiles had received the fulness of the gospel, the natural branches of the olive tree, or the remnants of the house of Israel, should be grafted in, or come to the knowledge of the true Messiah, their Lord and their Redeemer.
>
> 1 Nephi 10:14

I had always believed in the gospel. The Book of Mormon and the prophecies of Lehi and Nephi, Isaiah, and Helaman all were scriptures I believed. It is one thing to believe in a prophecy. To be a literal part of one, in real-time, is another thing entirely. Here, in just a few words, I learned that I was a literal part of the prophecy of Lehi. I was a remnant of the house of Israel, a literal child of Joseph, and grafting back in my family, the people of Barcelona, into the true vine.

I was part of scattered Israel and was being gathered. By becoming a Denning, I was able to be gathered. And now I was gathering my birth family.

Kinsman Redeemer

There is a role that we often overlook as those who have received the covenant. Blessings come with obligations. We are gifted the gospel of the Savior, priesthood, prosperity, posterity, and promised land, which also comes with obligations. We are blessed with so much that it is easy to forget the responsibilities we have to the family of the Lord. As children of Christ, brothers, and sisters in the gospel, we are responsible for our family. This is the role of the kinsman redeemer (Exodus 22:22, 23:6, 11; Leviticus 25:25, 35, 39, 47–8; Deuteronomy 10:18, 24:14, 17).

Save the Widow and Orphan

In Ancient Israel, there was a different form of "welfare." We are used to having social programs that, as a community, we support women, children, and those in need. Anciently, however, there were no safety nets, no social programs, and no help when bad things happened. Some groups were particularly vulnerable. Women and orphans had nowhere to go when things went wrong. Women in those days did not have many career opportunities. Instead, they relied on their fathers, then husbands for material support. If a husband died, leaving a widow, she had only family to turn to.

Often you see stories of widows and orphans in scripture. Judah's daughter-in-law, Tamar, was left without a husband and no support and appealed to Judah for help (Genesis 38). Ruth and Naomi, daughter-in-law and mother-in-law, lost their husbands and were in dire straits (see the book of Ruth). These stories tell of people with these challenges and the sacred duty we have to support them in these times.

It is similarly distressing to be without familial support in the New Testament. The story of the widow's mite shows how needy she is. Thus, her two mites, a tiny fraction of money, become a robust offering. Jesus raised the son of the widow of Nain, recognizing what it meant to her to have support. While a fantastic miracle of life over death, it is also a miracle of love, care, and rescue (Luke 7:11–17).

Jesus, while hanging on the cross, was concerned for his own dear mother, Mary.

> Now there stood by the cross of Jesus his mother, and his mother's sister, Mary the wife of Cleophas, and Mary Magdalene. When Jesus therefore saw his mother, and the disciple standing by, whom he loved, he saith unto his mother, Woman, behold thy son! Then saith he to the disciple, Behold thy mother! And from that hour that disciple took her unto his own home.
>
> John 19:25–27

The Lord has a special place in His heart for orphans and widows, and He is "a father of the fatherless, a defender of widows . . . in His holy habitation" (Psalm 68:5, NKJV).

Redeem the Slave

Another vulnerable group was the family member who had become a servant or enslaved person. This was sometimes because of poverty, and in those days, people sold themselves into slavery for a time to survive. The kindred redeemer was responsible for paying the price to release or redeem him. The word "redeem" means paying for or alleviating the debt (Leviticus 25:33, 27:15; Deuteronomy 10:18).* The irony of the story of Joseph of Egypt becomes more evident when we realize that the family—who would be responsable for redeeming him should he be enslaved—instead sold him into slavery.

Blessings Gifted to the Kinsman Redeemer

The kinsman redeemer was given material blessings to help support these requirements. They were given twice the portion of land and material wealth. This is often what the "firstborn son" was receiving from the father. The firstborn would get twice the land, the crops, the

---

* Richard Whitaker, Francis Brown, et al., *The Abridged Brown-Driver-Briggs Hebrew-English Lexicon of the Old Testament* (Boston; New York: Houghton, Mifflin and Company, 1906).

orchards, and material wealth so that if needed, they could support the family. The redeemer had to take on the debt, pay the price, and continue to care for those they had redeemed.† The kinsman redeemer received blessings and responsibilities to support, save, and redeem his family. The role of the kinsman redeemer was not just a one-time event, rather it went on for the lifetime of that family member. Once saved, the redeemer had responsibility for that family member forever.

Christ is the Kinsman Redeemer

Christ is the kinsman redeemer for all of us, sent to bring all into the family of God.

> But when the fulness of the time was come, God sent forth his Son, made of a woman, made under the law, to redeem them that were under the law, that we might receive the adoption of sons. And because ye are sons, God hath sent forth the Spirit of his Son into your hearts, crying, Abba, Father. Wherefore thou art no more a servant, but a son; and if a son, then an heir of God through Christ.
>
> Galatians 4:4–7

Paul tells us that we become his children in our covenant with Christ. We are not servants but a child of Christ and an heir to the kingdom. Christ redeems all of us and makes all of us His children. He is the great kinsman redeemer, sent to save all of us.‡

The kinsman redeemer is a title, a duty, and a responsibility. It is sometimes called just "redeemer," as in Isaiah:

> But now thus saith the Lord that created thee, O Jacob, and he that formed thee, O Israel, Fear not: for I have redeemed thee, I have called thee by thy name; thou art mine.

---

† Richard Whitaker, Francis Brown, et al., *The Abridged Brown-Driver-Briggs Hebrew-English Lexicon of the Old Testament* (Boston; New York: Houghton, Mifflin and Company, 1906).

‡ Douglas K. Stuart, *Exodus*, vol. 2, The New American Commentary (Nashville: Broadman and Holman Publishers, 2006), 261–26.

> [2] When thou passest through the waters, I will be with thee; and through the rivers, they shall not overflow thee: when thou walkest through the fire, thou shalt not be burned; neither shall the flame kindle upon thee. [3] For I am the Lord thy God, the Holy One of Israel, thy Saviour: I gave Egypt for thy ransom, Ethiopia and Seba for thee.
>
> [4] Since thou wast precious in my sight, thou hast been honourable, and I have loved thee: therefore will I give men for thee, and people for thy life. [5] Fear not: for I am with thee: I will bring thy seed from the east, and gather thee from the west;
>
> [6] I will say to the north, Give up; and to the south, Keep not back: bring my sons from far, and my daughters from the ends of the earth;
>
> [7] Even every one that is called by my name: for I have created him for my glory, I have formed him; yea, I have made him.
>
> Isaiah 43:1–7

The Lord connects three ideas here: love, redemption, and gathering. Here he explains that He loves us and remembers Israel, the covenant name for the family of Jacob. He loves us and remembers us. That is what He covenanted to do.

The blessing, the extra portion, meant you had additional responsibility in your family. Similarly, when the family of Abraham receives the blessing, they are intended to serve. Abraham is told, "and in thy seed shall all the nations of the earth be blessed; because thou has obeyed my voice" (Genesis 22:18). This call to serve and share the special blessing is the responsibility of the kinsman redeemer. This blessing and responsibility are extended to all covenant people.

At the top of Mount Sinai, after the Israelites have fled Egypt. This is the part of the story where the family of Abraham has been in bondage for hundreds of years in Egypt. The Lord raises up a deliverer Moses, to save them from bondage. After the plagues of Egypt, the Passover when God protected the firstborn, and the crossing of the Sea on dry ground, we reach the key event—Sinai.

At the culmination of the Exodus story, we have the Lord's invitation to become a holy nation, a peculiar people, a kingdom of priests and priestesses. The Lord invites us back into His presence to be His friends. He calls this being holy. We enter into a covenant to become specially set apart, consecrated to Him. We become extensions of His family. We become kinsmen.

We Are Kinsman Redeemers

As we covenant to become a consecrated people, we become a kinsman redeemer to all our family. We are given blessings so that we may, in turn, reach out to those family members who may need us. This may be in material blessings. It can also be a spiritual blessing. The gift of the Holy Spirit, a testimony of the Savior, and the benefits of the Holy priesthood are boundless. We are responsible for redeeming our brothers and sisters as we receive these things.

We are first redeemed. We come unto Christ and are perfected in Him. We are like the disciples of old, learning to become more like Him daily. Our covenant path is one of learning and changing. It may be a challenge, but we can set our sights on the Savior.

How Do We Gather Israel?

As we are scattered and gathered back into the Lord's arms, we are asked to become like Him. We begin to gather. We first remember who we are. As covenant Israel of the tribes of Jacob, we are given the same promises and responsibilities as the ancestors of old. We are called to gather Israel.

We can reach out to the One, like the Samaritan woman or the leper. We can help those in our own families, like Jacob or Esau. We may not know how to serve, but the Lord takes our offering, small or great, and makes it more. He takes what we give back to Him and make it miraculous. There are opportunities to serve formally, as a mission, and we may feel the call. We can help with the talents we are given. We serve and minister in our family, neighborhood, and ward.

Recalling again, President Russell M. Nelson declared, "*Anytime* you do *anything* that helps *anyone*—on either side of the veil—take a step toward making covenants with God and receiving their essential baptismal and temple ordinances, you are helping to gather Israel. It is as simple as that."* Our work in the kingdom is the gathering of Israel. Teaching a class, playing a hymn, serving a mission, preparing temple names, and serving in the House of the Lord are all gathering Israel.

You are the kinsman redeemer, modeled after our Lord Jesus Christ. We are blessed so that we may gather.

RETURN of the REMNANT

A Vision of Hope and Gathering

The prophet Jeremiah lived during the time of the Exile. Living during an exceptionally challenging time, he received a vision of the remnant who would be gathered. The Lord shares the vision for the gathering of Israel. He shares a vision of the amazing, blessed, and miraculous time in which we live, the time when all of Israel will once again be gathered. He shares what it is to be lost and scattered, found and gathered, and how we are all a remnant. The Lord will be the God of all the families of the Earth. We shall be His people.

At that time, says the Lord,
I will be the God of all the families of Israel, and they shall be my people.

[2] Thus says the Lord:
The people who survived the sword
found grace in the wilderness;
when Israel sought for rest,
[3] the Lord appeared to him from far away.
I have loved you with an everlasting love;
therefore I have continued my faithfulness to you.
[4] Again I will build you, and you shall be built,
O virgin Israel!
Again you shall take your tambourines,

---

* Russell M. Nelson, "Hope of Israel," worldwide devotional for youth, June 3, 2018, churchofjesuschrist.org/broadcasts, emphases added.

and go forth in the dance of the merrymakers.
5 Again you shall plant vineyards
on the mountains of Samaria;
the planters shall plant,
and shall enjoy the fruit.
6 For there shall be a day when sentinels will call
in the hill country of Ephraim:
"Come, let us go up to Zion,
to the Lord our God."

7 For thus says the Lord:
Sing aloud with gladness for Jacob,
and raise shouts for the chief of the nations;
proclaim, give praise, and say,
"Save, O Lord, your people,
the remnant of Israel."

8 See, I am going to bring them from the land of the north,
and gather them from the farthest parts of the earth,
among them the blind and the lame,
those with child and those in labor, together;
a great company, they shall return here.
9 With weeping they shall come,
and with consolations I will lead them back,
I will let them walk by brooks of water,
in a straight path in which they shall not stumble;
for I have become a father to Israel,
and Ephraim is my firstborn.

10 Hear the word of the Lord, O nations,
and declare it in the coastlands far away;
say, "He who scattered Israel will gather him,
and will keep him as a shepherd a flock."
11 For the Lord has ransomed Jacob,
and has redeemed him from hands too strong for him.
12 They shall come and sing aloud on the height of Zion,
and they shall be radiant over the goodness of the Lord,
over the grain, the wine, and the oil,

and over the young of the flock and the herd;
their life shall become like a watered garden,
and they shall never languish again.
13 Then shall the young women rejoice in the dance,
and the young men and the old shall be merry.
I will turn their mourning into joy,
I will comfort them, and give them gladness for sorrow.
14 I will give the priests their fill of fatness,
and my people shall be satisfied with my bounty,
says the Lord. . . .

20 Is Ephraim my dear son?
Is he the child I delight in?
As often as I speak against him,
I still remember him.
Therefore I am deeply moved for him;
I will surely have mercy on him,
says the Lord.

Jeremiah 31:1–14, 20, NRSV

About LORI DENNING

Lori Denning is a scripture nerd. She holds a bachelor's degree in biblical studies from Multnomah University, where she studied Hebrew and the Bible and was awarded highest honors. She holds a master's degree in theology from Gonzaga University.

Sister Denning has taught Gospel Doctrine classes as well as classes in the Church Educational System. She has a popular vlog, *The Bible Brief*, introducing books of the Bible to a wide audience. She also hosts a podcast, *:20 Minute Scriptorian*, which covers the Come, Follow Me curriculum. Her passion is sharing the gospel of Jesus Christ through His scriptures.

Lori served a mission in Barcelona, Spain, and currently resides in South Jordan, Utah.